QUAIL FARMING FOR BEGINNERS

THE ULTIMATE COMPREHENSIVE GUIDE

Copyright 2021, Karen June P

All rights reserved. No part of this book may be reproduced or transmitted in any form or by any means, electronic or mechanical, including photocopying, recording, or by any information storage and retrieval system, without written permission from the copyright owner.

Disclaimer

The contents of this book are for the intention of people meaning to raise quail as a hobby. The author accepts no responsibility for any loss or consequential loss as a result of relying on any advice contained herein.

External links

While there are links provided herein to third-party web sites, this has been done to provide convenience to the reader. The author does not control the third-party web sites and is not responsible for the contents of any linked-to, third-party web sites. The author does not endorse, recommend or approve any third-party web site hyperlinked from herein. The author bears no liability to any entity for the content, or use of the content from the hyperlinks. Since the owners of the sites may change their sites' addresses and content referenced from herein without notice, the author will accept no liability in case of such, or related scenarios.

All rights reserved

Acknowledgements

I would like to thank all the quail keepers, breeders, and veterinary personnel. Your in-depth evaluation, priceless corrections and incredible additions have made this book a gem to behold. To James, Nicholas, Steve, Shantel, Dan, Monica, Shane, Levis, Arthur, Mr. and Mrs. Johnson, may the Almighty God bless you abundantly!

Special Dedication

This book is dedicated to all quail keepers: aspiring keepers, beginners, and existing keepers. Everyone has something special to learn from the author's and other contributors' extensive experience and knowledge on quail.

CONTENTS

Chapter One

Quail, A Brief Summary..11
What is Quail Farming?..14
Where to Get Quail Eggs and Live Quail Bird.............15
What to Look Out for Before Buying Eggs and Live Quail..16

Chapter Two

Why You Should Consider Raising Quail..................20
Will Quail Disturb My Neighbours?..............................24

Chapter Three

How to Start Quail Farming...25
Market Research..26
Decide on Niche Area of Production........................27
Location..27
Business Name..28
Licensing Requirement...29
Insurance Policies..29
Sole Proprietorship Vs. Limited Liability Company........29
Possible Challenges...30
Starting From Scratch Vs Buying an Established Farm..31
Funding...31

Chapter Four

Housing..33
Things to Take Into Consideration When Housing Quail33
Space Requirements...35
Cages...36
Deep Litter System..38
Hutch..38
Height of the Housing..39
More Tips on Housing Quail...................................40

Chapter Five

Light and Temperature Management.......................43
Sexing..44

Chapter Six

Feeding Quail...46
Feed Proportions..47
Giving the Egg-Laying Birds Calcium.....................48
Kinds of Treats to Give Quail................................48
DIY – How to Breed Mealworms at Home..............49

Chapter Seven

Egg Production..52
Best Performing Strains of Quail...........................53
Most Common Quail Breeds for Egg and Meat
Production...53
Eggshell Colouring...55
Odd Sized Eggs...55
Collecting the Eggs..56

How to Deepen the Egg Yolk Colour.........................56
Egg Laying Problems – Causes and Possible Solutions...57
Prolapsed Vent..61
Causes of Vent Prolapse..61
How to Identify a Hen With Prolapsed Vent...............62
Treating a Prolapsed Vent...62

Chapter Eight

Egg Fertility...64
Egg Candling..64
Characteristics of Quail Eggs Suitable for Incubation....66
How to Validate Fertility of Incubated Eggs...............66
Taking Care of the Eggs Before Incubation................67
Float Testing Eggs to Determine the Level of Freshness.68

Chapter Nine

Incubation...69
How to Successfully Incubate Quail Eggs..................69
Temperature and Humidity...70
Turning the Eggs..71
Why Incubated Eggs May Fail to Hatch, and Possible Solutions for Each Case..72
Pipping...75
Pipped Eggs that Fail to Hatch...................................76
How to Float Test Eggs that Fail to Hatch..................76

Chapter Ten

Taking Care of Quail Chicks......................................78
Brooder...79

Temperature..79
Observing the Behavior of Chicks Inside the Brooder....80
Lighting..80
Bedding...80
Feed Management..81

Chapter Eleven

Quail Health..82
General Signs Exhibited by Sick Quail.........................82
What Makes Quail to Be Susceptible to Disease or Pest Infection..85
The Four Most Common Quail Diseases, Preventions and Treatments..86

Chapter Twelve

More on Quail Health..92
Bumblefoot..92
Treating Bumblefoot..93
Toe-Balling..94
Managing Toe-balling..94
Pest Management...95
Use of Permethrin..95
Use of Garlic..96
General Things You Can Do to Contain Quail Pests and Diseases...96
Use of Apple Cider Vinegar..98
DIY – How to Make Homemade Apple Cider Vinegar...99
Can You Give Baby Quail Apple Cider Vinegar?..........101
Summarized Key Benefits of Keeping Healthy Quail...101

Chapter Thirteen

General Care and Management............................102
How to Hold Quail..102
Taming Quail...103
Why Quail Fight and Possible Solutions for Each Case.104
Feather Plucking in Quail - Causes and Possible Solutions for Each Case..108
Pecking in Quail – Causes and Possible Solutions.......111
Egg-Eating in Quail...114
Causes of Egg-Eating...114
Identification...115
Control of Egg-Eating..116

Chapter Fourteen

Why Quail are Dying; Causes and Possible Solutions – Both Baby Quail and Adult Quail.........................117
Culling Quail – How to Butcher Quail....................123
Location of the Cull...124
Culling by Chopping Off the Head........................124

Chapter Fifteen

Branding, Sales and Marketing.............................126
How to Bolster Your Farm's Brand........................126
- Get professional certifications....................127
- Set favorable prices................................127
- Promote your farm.................................128

Simple Yet Effective Sales and Marketing Strategies...131

Chapter One

Quail, A Brief Summary

Quail are small sized birds in the order of *Galliformes.*

Quail are not poultry birds. They are game birds. Their preferred habitat consists of wild grasses, scrub, bush, forest, and sometimes open woodlands. They like hideaway places, though not so dark.

Compared with other poultry birds such as chicken of similar age, quail are small in both body size and weight. A mature adult bird has an average weight of 200grams.

They have little, yet sharp beaks that will peck at anything that catches their interest, and even sometimes for no apparent reason!

Nesting

In the wild, quail build a nest before laying or hatching their eggs. They lay 5-10 eggs, and sometimes even more, clutch them together in their nests and then sit on them. The male and female will take turns sitting on the eggs, and sometimes sitting on the eggs together.

Incubation

In their natural habitat, quail will sit on their eggs till hatching. And in the event the hen leaves or get killed, the male partner will successfully shoulder the responsibilities of sitting on the eggs till hatching, and that of raising the chicks.

Feeds and water

Compared with chickens, quail are very aggressive eaters – they have a vigorous drive to search for food. They are also fussy eaters, they eat rapidly.

In the wild, quail feed mostly on seeds, berries, fruits and insects. They forage along the ground and under grasses and bushes in search of the feeds.

Most quail species seldom fly. They instead prefer running along the ground, or when startled, take a quick vertical leap into the air (usually in a quick burst of light).

Quail must drink water daily or get it from their food. Did you know quail breed such as Gambel can simply eat insects and succulent fruits of cacti nature to get water?

Mating

With good husbandry, quail can live for more than 3 years.

When adult quail pair up and mate, they don't just do it for a single breeding season – they mate for life! They stay monogamous till death separate them – carrying out duties equally such as looking for nesting sites, building the nest, incubating eggs and raising the young ones.

Classification

Below is a closer look into the family tree of Quail.

Class: Aves *(birds)*
Order: Galliformes *(game birds and fowl)*
Family: Phasianidae *(Pheasants, Partridges and Quail)*
Genus: 13 different genera commonly split into two groups: *Old World* and *New World*.

Old World Quail: *Coturnix, Anurophasis, Perdicula, Ophrysia.*

New World Quail: *Dendrortyx, Oreortyx, Callipepla, Philortyx, Colinus, Odontophorus, Cyrtonyx, Rhynnchortyx, Dactylortyx*

What is Quail Farming?

Quail farming is simply the business of raising quail for either domestic or commercial production of eggs, meat, or both.

Due to their small-sized bodies, quail eat small amounts of feeds, occupy smaller spaces, and require little care and management.

In the recent times, the poultry industry has witnessed an increase in demand for both eggs and meat. Notably, increased health consciousness amongst world's meat consumers has bolstered the consumption of white meat with chickens, fish, and quail offering the majority share.

Compared with other poultry birds, quail farming continues to gain traction each new day across the world due to low capital and minimal labor demand, ease of care and management of the birds, and high profit returns. Interestingly, anyone can start the venture with both limited capital and limited experience!

Where to Get Quail Eggs and Live Quail Bird

Quail lay small-sized, multicolored eggs. The eggs tastes just like the chickens', although they have a slightly higher yolk to white.

You can get fertilized quail eggs, unfertilized eggs, or live birds from several places. You can get them from the local supermarkets, high-end markets, local whole food stores, grocery stores, and at the local farmers' markets.

You can do an online search to see if any quail owner or quail breeder lives near you. This will allow you get the products directly from the source.

Also, depending on where you live, you can order the eggs and live birds online from market places such as Amazon, Ebay, Spade and Feather, Stromberg's, Cackle Hatchery, McMurray Hatchery, Purely Poultry, Moonridge Farm, Manchester Farms, Preloved, WoodBottom Quail Farms, Wadley Quail Farm, Murano Hatchery, Meyer Hatchery etc.

What to Look Out for Before Buying Quail Eggs and Live Quail

Before buying any quail product, you should take into consideration the below, especially if your intention is not to make a meal once you arrive home, but want to either incubate the fertilized eggs, or raise the live birds.

- **Buy the products from reputable sellers**

    What's the credibility of the person selling you the products? Strive to buy from sellers with proven good reputation. Are there licensed reputable quail breeders or quail dealer outlets in your region? These are the people/places to give first preference when you decide to buy your first flock.

    Ask a few of your friends raising the birds to recommend to you credible sellers. In case you are buying online, do a thorough search and don't just trust the first seller you come across online and send them money immediately! Some online websites publicly show reviews of other buyers - rating the services/products on a scale of between 1 to 5. You can rely on such, plus your instinct to guide you accordingly.

- **How old are the eggs/birds?**

  Knowing the age of the birds is key to determining the type of care and feeds you'll give them. Fertile eggs usually have a shelf life of about 14-16 days, with incubation recommended to be started before the tenth day – if you want good results.

- **Establish the age of the birds that have produced the products**

  This is important to avoid experiencing low hatch rates and inbreeding problems. Quail that have stayed for more than two and half years may lay infertile eggs, those with low hatch rates, and resultant chicks with deformities. Ask the flock rotation or refreshment plan of the breeder (how frequent new flock is brought in). The more frequent they are brought in, the higher should be the quality of the products.

- **Avoid buying through the cold period**

  Naturally, quail lay inconsistently during winter, and in case they do, the eggs are usually of low quality. And unfortunately, you can never tell a good egg from a bad one from the outer shell!

- **Establish how they are packaged and sent**

    If buying online, it's important to know how the seller packages and sends – especially the fertilized eggs. This will help you judge whether the eggs will arrive in good condition (safe from damage or from exposure to excessive cold/heat), or not.

- **Inquire about the hatch rate of the eggs**

    The seller should be able to tell the estimated hatch rate for the fertilized eggs. Any hatch rate below 60% would not be ideal. If the hatch rate is say 70% and onwards, that would be most ideal.

- **For starters, get that firsthand experience**

    Visit at least three different local quail farms/breeders to see breeds available, how they are raised, and the production capabilities of the breeds.

- **Get the right birds**

    Avoid purchase of breeding flock with deformities or those of different sizes and different colors. They may not get along (may engage in endless fights), resulting into low, unprofitable outputs. Equally, establish the history of mortality or diseases of the breed you intend to purchase.

- **Start with one breed**

  At start, go with one type of breed. Avoid mixing different quail breeds as they may not be friendly to one another, especially if they are being raised in the same cages.

- **Get the right fertile eggs for incubation**

  If you decide to purchase quail eggs for incubation, insist on getting eggs with equal (similar) sizes, shapes and colors. Equally, buy eggs with no abnormality.

Incredible link for further reading

Quail Breeds and How To Pick The Right Bird For You*https://www.backyardchickens.com/articles/quail-breeds-and-how-to-pick-the-right-bird-for-you.67350/*

Chapter Two

Why You Should Consider Raising Quail

Quail grow and mature fast. They are ready to begin laying eggs at just between 6-8 weeks from hatching.

Below are some of the reasons why you should consider raising quail.

- **Perfect alternative for urban farms that can't keep chickens**

There are certain urban places that do not grant permits to the residents to raise poultry such as chicken, but might be having exceptions for quail. In fact, most have quail left out of their legislations altogether. Although quail may sing (make some low tone chirps and coos), that sound is less likely to be heard meters from their housing, thus would much less likely to disturb or annoy your neighbours, than a rooster's crow at dawn.

- **Quail lay eggs every day**

Coturnix quail, just like chickens, lay eggs daily. They lay spotted and speckled eggs. Raising them is therefore an opportunity to look forward to fresh, nutritious, delicious and adorable eggs each day. With supplemental lighting, they will lay eggs all year round.

- **They have quick turnaround time**

Fertile Coturnix quail eggs take between 15-17 days to hatch (when correctly incubated. From hatching, they take 6-8 weeks to attain maturity and start laying eggs. And on an interesting note, baby quail do fetch better prices than baby chickens, and quail eggs and meat have premium sales values.

Their meat is generally of good weight when butchered for the table. Notably, one to three birds can sufficiently feed anyone. They don't have any foul smell, and proccssing their meat take less time.

- **Quail adapt easily**

Quail can easily be raised alongside other poultry birds such as turkey, chicken, duck etc. due to their friendly personality. They equally adapt to most climate and weather conditions enabling them to be found in most parts of the world.

- **They don't take up much space**

Due to their small-sized bodies, you can raise an entire flock in a contained area such as a garage, outdoor shed or laundry room. A space the size of a square meter would be sufficient to raise eight to ten birds. That same space would only house just two to three chickens.

- **Low capital and labor investment requirement**

Quail are quiet easy to take care of. You'll only spare a few minutes a day to feed them, give them water, collect their eggs, or change their bedding. You need low capital investment to start raising them. Equally, the labor investment need is low.

- **Source of income and employment**

Just like any other business, quail farming provides an excellent source of income and a stable a source of employment to many people around the globe.

- **Quail are hardy**

Quail are a bit hardy. They are affected by fewer to no diseases when compared with poultry birds such as chicken. Quail do not get sick easily or frequently. As long as you raise them in the right environment and give them the necessary care and management they deserve, they'll register few to no health issues.

- **They have high feed conversion rate**

Compared with other poultry birds, quail have a high feed conversion rate. Roughly, they are able to produce 1 kg of meat out of 3 kgs of feeds.

- **Quail products are affordable**

Quail products: eggs and meat, are more affordable than those of other poultry birds such as turkey

- **Cheaper feeds**

Quail feeds are cheaper than most poultry feeds. Interestingly, they don't eat as much as chickens do, but need quality feeds for good production. For every 1lb of feeds, they lay 1 lb of eggs.

- **They produce tasty, rich, and delicious eggs and meat**

Quail eggs and meat are tastier and low in cholesterol than those of most poultry birds. Consequently, there is a high demand for the products at the markets and from most farm gates.

Research has pointed out that quail's egg has loads of vitamins, nutrients, and is low in caloric content. It has vitamin A (retinol), Vitamin B1, Vitamin B2, (riboflavin), Vitamin B6, Vitamin B12, Vitamin c, D, & E. It also has essential nutrients such as Omega 3, Potassium, Zinc, Iron, Phosphorus, choline, tonic acid, Magnesium, Omega 6, fatty acids and selenium.

Will Quail Disturb My Neighbours?

Some female quail may emit soft songs that seem to blend in with most songs made by many other birds. On the other hand, male quail will tend to emit an even louder song, but in all cases, the songs are not only pleasant but are also occasionally emitted, thus should not be a nuisance to your neighbours.

Link for further reading

Health benefits of quail eggs:
http://www.quailfarm.co.uk/index.php/quail-and-health

Chapter Three

How to Start Quail Farming

Start with a manageable flock to see if you'll like them. Quail are anything but consistent.

Many of us live in tight places such as flats or houses with small gardens, yet long to raise quail birds. The good news is, yes you can raise quail in any small contained area such as balcony, garage, patio or garden!

Raising quail for either domestic or commercial production of eggs and meat is not that involving. With some little capital and relevant infrastructure, you are ready to go. However, to profitably raise the birds, it's essential to first have in place a proper business plan. The plan will help you focus on a specific niche area of production - such as egg production, meat production, fertile eggs production, chicks production etc. The plan will also guide you in selecting the right breeds of quail to raise, the right ages of the birds to acquire, the kind of infrastructure to have in place, the sales and marketing strategy to adopt in order to reach your targeted market, etc. However, although having the business plan in place would be beneficial, it's not a must at start-up level. So it's up to you to decide whether to have a business plan or not.

Just like any other business venture, although quail farming has its own fair share of challenges, it's a truly profitable business venture. Yes, quail farming has been in existence for far too long, but the business isn't yet saturated. There is always a ready market for the birds' products, and depending on your financial status, you can decide to either start on a small scale or large scale.

Market Research

The initial step towards great quail farming is via carrying out thorough market research and feasibility study.

Although the consumption of quail eggs and meat is not restricted to a specific group of people, with people from all walks of life, different races and cultures consuming the products, it's essential to establish the actual demographics and psychographics of quail consumers in your area and in your intended market. Doing this will help you make the right decision on the actual size of your farm (large scale or small scale), the breeds of birds to raise, and the purpose of your production.

Decide on Niche Area of Production

Throughout the world, there are more than 18 different species of domestic quail available for raising. While some are suitable for egg production, others are good for meat production, and others perform best for both egg and meat production.

But broadly, there are just two types of quail breeds: broilers and layers. Broilers are raised for breeding and for meat production, with the most common ones being the *Bobwhite (American)*, and the *White Breasted (Indian)*. Layers on the other hand are raised for breeding and for egg production. The most common ones too are *the British Range, The English White, Tuxedo, Pharaoh,* and *the Manchurian Golden.*

Most players in the quail farming business have no specific niche area of focus. Many are simply raising the birds for production of eggs and meat. To be successful, you should clearly define your market and then focus all your energy towards delivering quality products to that market.

Location

Conduct thorough feasibility and market study to ensure your intended location is ideal - I guess you would not marvel at starting a quail farm in the exact location where another quail farm just closed shop a few days ago due to unsupportive regulations and, or due to lack of viable market!

The things to consider when choosing location for your quail farm should include:

- Demography of the area (the possible number of people living in that area).
- Demand of quail products in the area.
- Security and accessibility of the area.
- Level of competition in that area.
- Local regulations and laws covering the area.
- Purchasing power of the area's residents.

Since you'll have to shield the birds from any potential danger, you should also consider the below three things when deciding on the fencing need of your farm:

- Prevalent predators in the area
- Geographical composition of the area.
- Climatic condition of the area

Business Name

Be creative and give that proposed quail farm some catchy name. And never forget that most business names give the perception of what that business represents.

Licensing Requirement

Before you embark on raising quail, it's essential to get permit from relevant government authorities. In most cases, you'll be required to pay a small fee to be issued with the permit.

Since quail are game birds, check local, county and state guidelines on their possession and propagation.

Insurance Policies

In most countries including US, it's illegal to operate a business without having any form of basic insurance policy cover. You can consult an insurance agent/broker to guide you on ideal insurance cover for your business. Nonetheless, some of the possible insurance covers you should consider include: General insurance, Health insurance, Liability insurance, Farm equipment and auto insurance, Workers compensation insurance, birds' mortality insurance, Overhead expenses disability insurance, Business owners' policy group insurance, Payment protection insurance etc.

Sole Proprietorship Vs Limited Liability Company

You can start as a sole proprietor, general proprietor or as a limited liability company (LLC). If your focus is small scale, then sole proprietorship would be ideal.

Setting up an LLC on the other hand shields you from incurring personal liability. In the event of something going wrong with the operations, it's only the money you've invested in the company that will be at risk. Equally, you won't necessarily need board of directors, shareholders or other administrative formalities to get going. LLC are simpler and more flexible to operate.

Depending on your financial muscle and the scope of your intended operations, you can choose between Sole Proprietorship and Limited Liability Company.

Possible Challenges

Just like any other business venture, if you decide to start your own quail farming business today, you'll definitely be met with some threats or challenges. While some of the challenges may seem surmountable, others may appear totally insurmountable, leaving you with nothing to do other than remaining optimistic that sooner or later, things may turn around.

Some of the possible challenges you might face include:

- Competition from already established quail farms (to overcome this, you'll have to create your own market share of households, individuals, restaurants and hotels in need of supply of quail products).
- Emergence of a new competitor in the same location.
- Vandalism.
- Natural disasters such as bad weather.
- Unfavorable government policies.

Starting From Scratch Vs Buying an Established Farm

Since you'll seldom find a quail farm to purchase, you should prepare to start your own from scratch. It's less stressful starting from the scratch unlike buying one that will require you to carry out endless background checks.

To start from scratch, all you need is to get licensed, pull your startup capital, decide on ideal location, establish rapport with existing key stakeholders, utilize marketing tools to create awareness and then market your products.

Funding

You'll need adequate capital to acquire a piece of land, construct secure housing/cages, get the first set of quail chicks, feeds, and other relevant quail farming tools and equipment.

The level of amount of funds you'll need would depend upon the scale of your operation (large scale would be more capital intensive compared to small scale).

The first step towards securing funding from sources such as banks and investors is via writing a convincing business plan. Here below are some of the possible sources of funding to consider:

- From personal savings.
- Contributions from family members and friends.

- Sale of personal stocks and properties.
- Contributions from investors and business partners
- Sale of shares to interested investors.
- Soft loan from close family members and friends.
- Pitching the business idea and applying for seed capital and grants from angel investors, donors and from the government.

Chapter Four

Housing

The type of housing and its location plays a vital role in determining the performance quail.

Inspect the housing occasionally and fix any holes or cracks. Such may allow small predators like snakes and birds to attack quail. Equally, quail can get through small spaces and escape, or end up trapped.

Things to Take Into Consideration When Housing Quail

- **Pick a good housing system**

    Correct housing makes the birds less prone to behavioral issues, leading happier lives, and becoming highly productive. When raising the birds on a small scale, you can consider using cages or open space (deep litter system). But when raising them on a large scale, it's advisable to use cages. The cages will ensure you use little care and management as compared to use of deep litter.

- **Safety and security**

   The performance of quail is negatively affected by exposure to predators such as cats, dogs, rats, raccoons, snakes, other birds etc. These predators not only stress and scare the birds, they also prohibit quail from feeding and drinking well, thus lowering their productivity.

- **Adequate access to fresh air and light**

   Ensure the birds' accommodation has proper ventilation and with the right amount of exposure to light. Notably, exposure to light excites the birds, making them improve their performance.

- **Right space**

   To avoid stressing the birds, ensure they are raised in a right structure with adequate spaces, (though you may want to limit their movements within the accommodation to enable them put some weight – especially the broilers).

   The birds need adequate space to move to the feeders and waterers.

- **Limit their disturbance**

    Place their housing in a low-traffic area where the birds can't easily be disturbed unless it's necessary - such as when feeding, collecting eggs, or cleaning. Equally, keep other pets out of the same room as quail and ensure no young children can frequently go into the room and play with the quail.

- **Proper care and management**

    The housing should provide proper shelter from rain and hot sun. The food and water should be properly covered against downpours. The feeders and waterers should be adequate and put in clean, secure and convenient places where the birds can easily access them, and away from reach of rodents like rats and mice.

    The housing should be clean and neat to prevent the birds from contracting dirt related diseases like ulcerative enteritis. Cockroaches too can be a problem if the cage isn't kept clean. When housing the birds in tiered cages, you can construct the bottom of the cages with removable wooden plates to help in quick clearing of the birds' wastes.

Space Requirements

The space requirement depends on the type of housing. Under deep litter system, each adult bird would require

200-250square cm. And in the cages, each adult bird would require 150-175square cm.

Cages

You don't necessarily need an overly robust cage for the birds! You can either construct the cages on your own or buy commercially available ones from local vet shops and dealers.

Use of cages has numerous benefits including helping the birds gain desirable body weight - since unnecessary wandering is limited.

If using a space of say 150square cm per bird, for say 100 quail, the space requirement would be:

100 X 150 = 15,000 square cm.

This can be converted in a cage size of 150cm long and 100 cm wide.

And for say 50 quail, the space requirement would be:

50 X 150 = 7,500 square cm.

This too can be converted in a cage size of 100 cm long and 75 cm wide.

Don't be limited to any specific shape and size. The cages can be designed in various shapes and sizes. At 3-4 weeks, a cage size of 4ft X 2.5ft X 1.5ft can comfortably accommodate 100-120 quail, and at 5 weeks and onwards, the same space can accommodate ¾ of that number.

A unit of a cage can be 6ft in length and 1 feet wide. You can then divide this further into six isolated sub-units.

In the event you have limited space, you can arrange the cages in tiers, as high as four to six tiers. And also depending on available space, you can have any number of cages in a row (4, 5, ….).

You can construct the floor of the cages with ¼ wire mesh. This will not only allow the birds to move with ease on the surface, but will also allow their droppings to fall to the ground (or to the collection tray), thus limiting contamination and spread of quail's most common diseases like ulcerative enteritis.

The bottom of the cage should be sturdy enough to prevent the birds from caving in, and to equally bar animals like cats, dogs, raccoons, skunks, and rats from breaking in. Also ensure no predator can dig through the cage (from underground or from any side of the cage). You can add some wiring at the bottom of the cage and also all around the cage.

The cages should have proper ventilation.

For feeding, place long narrow feed troughs in front of the cages, and have the water troughs placed at the back of the cages.

Deep Litter System

This is a system of raising the birds on an open floor space, in specially constructed houses, pens or hutches.

To calculate the space requirement for say 100 birds under free range system, the space requirement of each quail would be 250square cm.

The space requirement for the 100 quail would therefore be (250X100) = 25,000 square cm.

You can then convert this into an ideal room set up of 250cmX100cm (250 cm long and 100 cm wide).

For say 50 quail, the space requirement would be: 250 X 50 = 12,500 square cm.

You can also break this into an ideal room set up of 125cm X 100cm (12cm long and 100cm wide).

Hutch

On a small scale, you can buy or convert an existing rabbit hutch into a perfect house for quail. A hutch for a single rabbit can comfortably house half dozen quail, but you must give special consideration to the fact that quail love exposure to light and some cover in which to hide, and to lay their eggs. You can, if using a rabbit hutch, make three windows on the side of the hutch to allow in more light.

Although chicken's housing would be ideal, it's would be a waste especially if looking to preserve space. Quail prefer a habitat much closer to that of a pheasant than a chicken. The birds too don't need elaborate nests. They prefer laying eggs in discreet places on their bedding – but they will always appreciate somewhere dark to lay the eggs.

Use sieved dry wood shavings as the bedding of the accommodation. The sieving is important to help eliminate as many dusts as possible. At times, some birds may confuse the dust with their feeds and peck on it. This may either chock/suffocate them or make them get sick .

Height of the Housing

The height of the housing would depend upon a number of things including: available space, the type of housing, the number of birds to be housed, and also whether the owner intends to go inside to perform daily chores like feeding and cleaning.

You can have the height at 6 feet if you intend to enter the room – though this would be a waste of viable space.

For the cages, you can have a height of at least 25 cm for the birds to move around freely. You should then fix a 5cm tray below each cage for collection of quail waste. Resultantly, a height of 30cm would be ideal for each cage. You can therefore have three cages comfortably fitted per one meter – but you can also spoil the birds with more space by having just two cages per meter.

More Tips on Housing Quail

- Give them more protection during the colder winter months (when the temperatures are approaching zero and below). You can move their accommodation into a contained warm area like a garage, or into some unutilized secure room in the house. But if outside, add in some extra inches of bedding material, and cover the walls of the cage with an old sack – while ensuring there is adequate ventilation. You can also introduce heat lamp.

- Ensure the birds are equally shielded from exposure to strong winds.

- The birds can fly short distances, so don't let them out of their enclosure.

- For commercial egg production, you can consider housing the females in colonies of 10-12 in each cage, and for breeding purposes, house the birds in the ratio of 1 male to 3-4 females.

- If a wire is used on the sides and at the bottom of the cage, the spacing should not be too big to allow predators to disturb quail.

- Inspect the housing occasionally and fix any holes or cracks. Such may allow small predators like snakes and birds to disturb quail. Equally, quail can get through small spaces and escape, or end up trapped.

- When the housing is placed outdoors, ensure it has a flat, non-mesh roof to bar quail from seeing birds flying in the sky. Seeing the flying birds may get them distracted and scared most of the time.

- Avoid use of structures that have open mesh on all sides (including the roofing). Quail are naturally shy and generally wary of movements over their head. They'll easily duck for cover when startled - in order to feel safe. They like to hide a lot; they do feel threatened when exposed. They prefer some corners and covers in which to hide in case they sense any danger. They would therefore feel safer in structures with some hide outs than in open structures.

- You can slightly slope the cage for the eggs to conveniently roll to the edge where they can be collected.

- Quail can be kept with or without a run – simply give them grass or other greens like vegetable in their diet.

- Perches and ramps would be wasted on them too. They like spending their time on the ground, never keen on climbing things.

- Always approach their housing slowly, giving them time to scurry off elsewhere. When startled, they are usually at risk of damaging their heads on the roof or on any loose hanging wire as they will attempt jumping up in response. They will however get used to you with time. You can stretch a soft net like fruit net or any other soft material just below the roof of their accommodation to contain their head-hitting impact.

Links for further reading

1. Step by step guide on building a quail hutch
https://www.instructables.com/id/Build-A-Quail-Hutch/

2. Low Budget Simple Quail Cage for 12 Japanese Quailhttp://www.quailfarm.co.uk/index.php/quail-info/22-low-budget-simple-quail-cage-for-12-japanese-quail

3. 18 DIY Quail Hutch Ideas And Designshttp://homestead-and-survival.com/18-diy-quail-hutch-ideas-and-designs/

4. How to Build a Quail Habitat
https://www.wikihow.com/Build-a-Quail-Habitat

Chapter Five

Light and Temperature Management

This section highlights in summary how to manage light and temperature for baby chicks (first week) to adult birds.

During the first week, maintain the temperature at 36.5^0C, lowering it down by 5^0C in the second week, a further 5^0C in the third week, and another 5^0C in the fourth week. You can then withdraw the heating bulb and let the birds use the room's temperature thereafter.

In terms of exposure to light, during the 1st and 2nd week, grant the chicks 24-hour access to light. In the 3rd to 5th week, you can limit that exposure by half (12-13 hours a day).

When they approach egg laying week (6th week and onwards), you can gradually start increasing the exposure from 12-13hours to 14-15 hours from the 6th week, 15-16hours from the 7th week, then 17-18 hours from the 8th week and onwards.

Sexing

This is the ability to differentiate a female quail from a male one. If you intend to raise quail for either egg or meat production, you must be able to tell the males and females apart.

Below are some simple ways of telling whether that quail is male or female:

Physical appearance
When mature, female quail appear slightly bigger in size than the male quail of the same age and breed.

Examining quail's vent/cloacae
There are two ways of examining the vent. First, when you press the area around it with two fingers, a small ball-like lump may pop forward suggesting the bird is male. If the ball-like lump fails to show up, that bird is possibly female. Also, when you press the vent, you may see presence of some white foam coming out of it, suggesting the bird is male. That foam also shows the bird is fertile, but is absent in female quail.

Roosting of the birds
Female quail are generally difficult to sex when young, but males will mostly start calling as they mature. At 4-5 weeks and onwards, male quail may begin roosting

By checking the color pattern on quail' chests
Female quail have speckled feathers on their chests while male quail have plain feathered chests. However, this method is only applicable on quail which have already grown enough feathers; usually at three weeks old and onwards. It is also effective on quail with speckled feathers like the Cortunix.

For Japanese quail, the male have a somehow reddish-brown chest feathers as they approach the 3rd week. And when mature, they produce 'foam-like-balls' (which originates from cloacal glands) showing they are fertile.

Links for further reading

1. Quail Farming – Vikaspedia
http://vikaspedia.in/agriculture/poultry/quail-farming

2. Photostimulation of Japanese quail
https://academic.oup.com/ps/article/94/2/156/1518598

3. How to get quails to lay eggs
https://www.roysfarm.com/how-to-get-quails-to-lay-eggs/

4. Lighting for quails to lay eggs
https://www.backyardchickens.com/threads/lighting-for-quails-to-lay-eggs.934024/

Chapter Six

Feeding Quail

Quail are great feeders who know when to stop. They will seldom over-eat!

In order to raise vibrant and productive quail, you must take the care and feeding of the birds seriously. Ensure they are well fed on balanced, nutritious, and sufficient feeds' all the time. Quail need balanced feeds to ensure they grow stronger and healthy, and attain desirable body weight.

Give them finely ground feeds rich in protein- since they have small-sized beaks.

Quail will seldom over-eat, so you should never worry about over-feeding them. An adult bird consumes roughly between 15-25g of food each day.

To avoid the hustle surrounding the making of homemade feeds, you can purchase commercial feeds (for any age group) found in most local vet stores.

From between $4_{1/2}$ to 7-8months, gradually change their feeds to grower/finisher ration. And due to high protein demand, turkey feed would be most ideal.

From the 8th - 9th week, those being raised for eggs or breeding should be put on breeders feed, with 20% of protein.

You may find some quail feeds having a mixed up of seeds and pellets. In their natural habitat, quail are known to thrive on feeding on a variety of seeds and cereals.

The birds can easily feed on other poultry feeds (chicken feeds, game bird feeds, etc.), but you must ensure such feeds have the right composition of protein (high content).

Feed Proportions

You can feed them on broken wheat, rice bran, sesame cake, broken oyster shell, fish meal, and mineral mix in the below proportions.

Ingredient	1st 3 Weeks (%)	4-6 Weeks (%)	6 Weeks Plus (%)
Broken wheat	47	49	50
Sesame cake	22	21	20

Fish Meal	20	18	16
Rice Bran	6	8	9
Finely broken Oyster Shells	2.5	3.5	4.5
Salt & Mineral Mix	0.5	0.5	0.5
Total	100	100	100

The layers require an average of 440-460 grams of feeds to lay 10 to 13 eggs.

Giving the Egg-Laying Birds Calcium

Calcium necessitates the laying of firm-shelled eggs. You can give them crushed oyster shells or dried and crushed egg shells. Give them the calcium in a separate bowl so that the males don't necessarily feed on it too.

Link for further reading

Housing And Feeding Your Quailhttps://www.backyardchickens.com/articles/housing-and-feeding-your-quail.67371/

Kinds of Treats to Give Quail

Give the birds a variety of treat and take your time to observe what they like and what they don't like.

- Live worms and insects – mealworms, woodlice, millipedes, spiders (small sized), earthworms
- Vegetable treats - broccoli leaves, cucumber, spinach, salad leaves etc.
- Scraps - boiled eggs, pasta, cereal, rice, bread
- Fruits - Strawberries, watermelon, pear, apple, peach, tomatoes etc.
- Give the birds a tub of sand for dust-bathing. Dust bathing not only helps in keeping the birds busy, it also helps in controlling mites, lice, and other external parasites.

  When the sand box is introduced for the very first time, the birds may be slow to embrace it. But given time, it will turn into a favorite spot.

Note: Do not feed them on avocado, uncooked potatoes, uncooked egg, stems and leaves of tomato plants, alcohol, wine or salty treats. These can be toxic to quail.

DIY - How to Breed Mealworms at Home

Breeding mealworms to give as treats to quail is very simple. To kick you off, let me first give you some few general details on mealworms.

The life circle of mealworms starts from eggs - laid by female darkling beetles. The eggs hatch into some tiny mini worms, then to molted worms, then to large worms, and then to pupae. The pupae eventually grow into young beetle, and the young beetle finally matures into an adult beetle.

You can therefore start breeding the worms using female darkling beetles, or molted/large mealworms. The beetles lay hundreds of tiny eggs (white in colour and oval in shape), which usually hatch in about 4 -20 days (in about two weeks) under ideal conditions. The eggs hatch into some tiny white larvae. You should therefore plan on moving the beetles every two weeks.

To maximize their growth, raise them under temperatures ranging between $72\text{-}81^0F$. Temperatures above 85^0F negatively interfere with their growth and development (may thwart their pupation).

Here is how to breed mealworms

- ✓ Get a plastic or glass container (small-sized to medium sized – depending on the number of birds you are keeping). The container should have smooth straight sides to bar the worms from climbing out.

- ✓ Since mealworms feed on grains and cereals, get some chick crumbles, corn flakes or bran flakes, or any other high protein poultry meal to form a substrate and put it at the bottom of the plastic container. The substrate should be finely ground to allow easy picking of mealworms and beetles when moving them.

- ✓ Get or buy some mealworms (live and healthy) from local breeders, vet shops, or from online platforms such as eBay. Once you receive the worms, put them inside the container, on top of the substrate.

- ✓ Then get some moisture food such as carrot peels, banana peels, apple, or potato and put inside the container. Avoid use of moisture food that contain a lot of water, or tight sealing on top of the container as the two will promote growth of mold

- ✓ With time, add in more poultry crumbles and more moisture food. As the mealworms keep feeding and growing, they'll be shading their exoskeletons, and also excreting sand-like substance, which may begin piling up in the container. You can blow away their exoskeletons – they are usually brown-like, dry and light. But when the sand-like substance (their poop) becomes too much, you can consider starting a new colony.

You'll always find plenty of worms beneath the moisture food – on top of the crumbles. The birds will appreciate being fed on freshly molted worms (the white coloured ones) since they have soft exoskeletons.

Since adult beetles can easily fly away, you can use a screen top to keep them in the container. The growth rate of worms will be dependent on temperature. Warmer weather stimulates faster growth while colder weather yields retarded growth.

Link for further reading: How to Breed Mealworms
https://www.wikihow.com/Breed-Mealworms

Chapter Seven

Egg Production

Quail are prolific egg layers. Each hen has the potential of laying at least an egg a day.

Compared with chickens that take 18-22 weeks to begin laying eggs, quail are ready to start laying eggs between the 6th and 8th week, and are into full egg production a week later!

At their best, when kept in the right conditions, given adequate and relevant feeds, exposed to right amounts of light, and shielded from cold and drought, quail have the potential of laying more than 250 eggs a year.

They will lay well for $1_{1/2}$ years, then register a slowdown thereafter. But with good care and management, they can lay well for up to 2 years.

They mostly lay in the afternoon and during evenings (when they are already well fed, relaxed, and are enjoying adequate exposure to light – when excited).

Note: Presence of male is not a necessity for the hens to lay eggs. However, presence of male is a necessity for the hens to lay fertilized eggs.

Best Performing Strains of Quail

The choice of quail bird to raise will depend upon your need of production – whether you want to keep the birds for egg or meat production, or both.

Did you know Japanese quail are the basis for most of the egg and meat producing quail? And since there is no known established official registration for breeding or naming, there are numerous variations in the names, colours, and size combinations given to them.

Most Common Quail Breeds for Egg and Meat Production

Texas A&M
This breed was originally bred by USA's Texas A&M College. They physically appear slightly larger than the Japanese quail, and are covered in pure white feathers.

Although they do lay eggs, they are primarily a meat bird. Their average size is 18-23cm(7-9inches).

British Range
With an average size of 15-18cm(6-8inches), the British Range are proven great egg layers and excellent table birds.

The English White
Just like the British Range, the English White are great egg layers and ideal table birds. Physically, their average size is 15-18cm (6-8inches).

Jumbo Japanese
With an average size of between 18-20cm(7-8inches), the Jumbo Japanese are ideal for the table and for egg laying.

Normal Japanese
They average 15-18cm(6-8inches) in size, and are known great egg layers and ideal table birds.

Italian
At 13-15cm(5-6inches), the Italian appears slightly smaller than the Japanese, but are good egg layers and table birds

Spanish
Also at 13cm-15cm(5-6inches), the Spanish are largely raised as egg layers, and are also small but delicious table birds.

Tuxedo

At 15-18cm(6-8inches), the Tuxedo are also great egg layers and good table birds.

In terms of taste, a quail egg is similar to chicken's, but with a softer texture and is less rubbery. Further, the eggs offer perfect alternatives to receipts in which you would normally use chicken's egg.

Eggshell Colouring

Quail eggs are cream-coloured with brown-like speckles. And in terms of egg shell pattering, there are endless variations.

Odd-Sized Eggs

There are chances you'll encounter double sized, soft-shelled, or extra small sized eggs. Such could occur when the birds are sick, stressed, or when they begin laying eggs. But if the trend continues, observe the birds closely, eliminating sickness, stress, or any likely cause.

Collecting the Eggs

Collect the eggs regularly, at least twice a day. Once collected, store the eggs with pointed ends facing downwards. I normally use an ice-cube tray to both collect and store the eggs. Quail eggs perfectly fit into the compartments of the ice-cube tray. You can also consider purchasing special miniature egg boxes from local poultry stores.

How to Deepen the Egg Yolk Colour

The eggs laid by healthy hens should have bright and bold orange yolks. Interestingly, the deeper the colour, the healthier the hens are.

Hens put on nutritious and well balanced diet lay eggs whose yolks are darker, fuller and thicker, and the egg shells are denser and harder to crack.

To deepen the egg yolk colour, give the birds treats rich in lutein, a xanthophyll which is found in plenty in green leafy vegetables such as kale, spinach and yellow carrots. The darker the greens the darker the yolk.

And don't forget to give the layers adequate calcium. If the laying hens do not get enough calcium, their bodies will extract the calcium from their bones and this may not be good. Give them crushed oyster shell (you can buy this from where you buy the feeds), or you can feed them their own crushed egg shells.

Egg Laying Problems – Causes and Possible Solutions

Sometimes you might think you are raising the birds accordingly; housing them accordingly, giving them the right feeds, ensuring they have access to clean water, giving them special treats like mealworms and vegetables, exposing them to extended lighting (at least 14 hours a day), housing the right number of males with females etc. only to be rewarded with egg laying challenges that include delayed egg laying, the birds failing to lay at all, the birds begin egg laying then the numbers starts dwindling afterwards, the birds begin laying then stop almost immediately, the birds skips egg laying on certain days, or the birds lay odd shaped/sized eggs.

Such experience may leave many quail owners powerless, forcing them to either sell or slaughter the affected birds. However, before making such decision, it's important to understand why quail would face challenges related to egg laying, especially once they attain the egg age, and how to mitigate such problems once they surface.

Quail may have trouble laying eggs due to certain reasons, which may include any of the below:

- They won't lay eggs before reaching the egg laying age.
- If they are housed in an insecure housing – where they are exposed to predators and domestic animals like cats, dogs, foxes, snakes etc. Equally, inhumane handling does scare quail, and tampers with their productivity.
- When given insufficient amounts of nutritious feeds and clean water.
- Due to sudden change in a normal routine i.e. change of time of filling the feeders and waterers, change in the quantity of feeds, change in the type of feeds, change in the feed/water locations, change of the feed bowls/water troughs, or even change of the person attending to them (yes quail are that sensitive!).
- Introduction of new bird in their housing.
- Disturbance from male birds (in case the males outnumber the females).
- Due to any other form of stress or sickness. A stressed hen may sit for a long time without laying an egg.
- Exposure to inadequate amount of light
- Aging of the birds

- Sudden change in environment i.e. moving their housing to a new location.
- Due to genetics (some quail may take up to 15 weeks to begin laying eggs).
- Uncomfortable place to lay the eggs.

Possible Solutions to Egg-Laying Challenges

➢ Ensure the birds' accommodation is safe and secure from access by predators and domestic pets. Locate the accommodation in a disturbance-free area.

➢ Give the birds the right feeds (that has the right content of protein). Some quail owners are usually tempted to put the layers on game bird starter or turkey starter forever! Well, the two might be ideal, but the starter feeds don't have enough calcium. You should therefore supply them with extra calcium – and this is where the oyster shells or their own dried egg shells come in handy. Ensure you grind them finely, and either mix with the feeds or put in a separate bowl.

➢ Avoid drastic changes in normal routine (sudden change in what they are used to). Once they begin laying eggs, avoid sudden change in type of feed. This might sound tricky when you want to switch from chick starter to layers feed, but the best way to do this is to gradually introduce the layers feed (a little of it mixed with chick starter) on the fourth week, and then have them on full layers feed from the sixth week and onwards.

- Always raise quail breed that has proven good egg-laying potential, and give them sufficient amounts of feeds and clean water all the time.

- Let the birds enjoy at least 14 hours of exposure to light each 24 hours.

- Always handle the birds as humanely as you possibly can. Doing this will keep them relaxed.

- House the right number of males with females. Although presence or absence of males has no impact on egg laying, when the males outnumber the females, they may turn into a nuisance, disturbing the females left and right, and thus lowering their egg laying potential. To get fertilized eggs, a ratio of 1 male to 3-4 females would be ideal.

- Treat sick birds in a timely manner and limit the birds' exposure to things that might stress them such as prolonged absence of feeds, frequent bringing in of new birds in the housing, putting on clothes that have clear pictures of predators and domestic pets like snake, dog, cat, fox etc.

- Keep differently aged birds separately. This is vital to help bar younger birds from being bullied by older birds.

Prolapsed Vent

Prolapsed vent is also known as cloacal prolapse or vent prolapse. It's a condition where the inner tissues of quail's cloaca protrude (hang out) from its vent, exposing the intestines, cloaca or uterus. In other words, it's essentially the insides sticking out.

The internal reproductive tract becomes loose and protrude from the vent, making passing of eggs and poop not only painful, but also potentially fatal!

While it's normal for the vent to prolapse when egg laying, it is abnormal for it to stay that way afterwards.

Causes of Vent Prolapse

- **Oversized eggs**
  Continual laying of oversized eggs may weaken or damage the hen's muscle tissue, leading to cloaca prolapse.

- **Overweight/underweight**
  Overweight and underweight hens are at risk to vent prolapse.

- **Disease infection**
  Vent prolapse can sometimes occur as a result of some infection in quail's abdomen or oviduct.

- **Lack of necessary nutrients**

Some studies suggest hens lacking calcium and magnesium may easily develop vent prolapse.

- **Younger birds/older birds**
  Young hens trying to lay large eggs, and older hens that have lost muscle tone are at risk to vent prolapse.

How to Identify a Hen With Prolapsed Vent

During the initial stages, it may be hard telling a hen developing prolapsed vent – if it's not exhibiting any amount of exposed tissue. You should therefore know your flock.

You can occasionally hold the hens and gently turn them upside down, one by one, while inspecting their vent area. You'll see externally exposed tissues from the birds suffering from vent prolapse.

Look out for change of behavior, signs of stress and any unusual occurrence such as lack of egg laying, reduced/lack of appetite, listlessness, bloody eggs, victim of bullying by other birds, endless fluffing of feathers etc.

Treating a Prolapsed Vent

The early you can identify the condition, the higher the chances of treating and preventing its re-occurrence.

The initial step is identifying the bird with vent prolapse, then separate it from the rest of the flock. Move it to some isolated place – like a special cage for the sick birds.

Prepare some warm bath and add in a little iodine – to help disinfect the area. Once ready, pour it in an open container, then hold the hen gently and put its back in the warm water. Doing so will help loose and wash away any stuck poop, clean any abrasions to the affected tissue, and also help hydrate and soften any loose tissue – these are necessary to ease reinsertion.

Use a water based lubricant to lubricate your fingers, or wear some gloves, then gently push the hanging tissue back in the vent. Be very slow, and very gentle!

If the tissue is swollen, you can use preparation H (available from most local stores), honey, or sugar to help relieve the swelling. Slowly and gently wipe the swelling with preparation H, honey, or sugar dissolved in warm water.

If there are abrasion or any chance of internal infection, consult trained veterinary personnel in your area for recommendation on the best antibiotic to administer. Don't do this on your own!

Ensure the hen gets enough calcium, magnesium, protein and vitamins.

Delay egg laying to allow the hen fully recover. You can continue holding it in the isolated room/cage, limit its activities and ensure it enjoys disturbance-free rest.

Note: In case your efforts don't work and the hen is still in pain, you can consider euthanizing it, humanely, to help it relieve the unending pain.

Chapter Eight

Egg Fertility

Before presenting quail eggs for incubation, it can be a tough task for an average quail farmer to tell a normal and fertile quail egg from an abnormal/infertile one. Generally, it would be heart-wrenching to incubate infertile quail eggs and wait for the hatching to occur!

Egg Candling

Egg candling is a simple act of examining an egg with an aim of detecting any defect or abnormality. The egg is viewed against a source of light like torch, sunlight, candle, or a specially designed candling lamp.

Some of the most common egg abnormalities that can be detected through candling include:

- ✓ Cracks on the eggshell.
- ✓ Absence of egg yolk.
- ✓ Presence of double yolk.
- ✓ Soft eggshells / very thin eggshells.
- ✓ Dark spots/blood spots/bloody ring around/in the egg.

Soft eggshell maybe a resultant of the hen prematurely laying the egg. It symbolizes lack of calcification in the egg which ought to have taken place in the shell gland. On the other hand, thin eggshells may symbolize disease infection, or some nutritional disorder.

The presence of blood clots or blood spots in an egg is a sign of broken blood capillaries during ovulation. An egg with such characteristics is unfit for incubation.

The color of a normal egg yolk ought to be yellow (normal, light or dark). Any deviation from this may be a sign of an abnormality, and may render the egg unfit for both incubation and even consumption.

The absence of an egg yolk or presence of a double yolk in an egg would render it unfit for incubation.

Characteristics of Quail Eggs Suitable for Incubation

- ✓ Should be oval in shape.
- ✓ Should have a single yolk, centered and yellowish (normal, light or dark).
- ✓ Clean with a clear and firm eggshell (free from cracks).
- ✓ Should possess clear yet thick and firm albumen.
- ✓ Free of blood spots/meat spots around, or in the egg yolk.
- ✓ Should be eight days old and below.

How to Validate Fertility of Incubated Eggs

The first step towards ensuring an egg laid by a quail bird is fertile is through correct pairing of the birds: one male to a maximum of 3-4 females.

On the seventh day of incubation, you can again candle the eggs. A fertile egg will exhibit a reddish embryo while an infertile one will show a clear embryo.

But if you can't tell the colors on the seventh day, you can again candle the eggs on the 13th or 14th day of incubation. If the chick is absent, you will observe a larger section of the egg containing a clear embryo, with minimal space left for air. But if the chick is present, the embryo will appear darker in color, or the light may not be able to penetrate through the eggshell.

Note: Always take lots of precaution when candling quail eggs since they have a delicate eggshell. Avoid candling the eggs against devices with strong or hot flames.

Taking Care of the Eggs Before Incubation

Collect the eggs daily, two to three times a day. This is necessary to prevent the eggs from accidental cracking, getting dirty, losing their shell moisture content, and to also to bar the birds from trying to peck at them.

Always handle the eggs with utmost care as they have a delicate outer shell layer.

Avoid washing any egg for incubation (especially the dirty eggs) since you may end up blocking the natural egg protective layers and expose the egg to entry by organisms. Simply put the dirty eggs aside, or wash them for consumption.

Store the eggs under correct temperature with suitable levels of humidity. Temperatures of $13\text{-}19^0C$ or $55\text{-}65^0F$ are ideal. Days before incubation, avoid storing the eggs in a refrigerator or at ordinary room temperature.

Ensure the fertile eggs are incubated at 7 or 8 days and below from the day they are laid. Avoid incubating eggs older than 10 days, they have a low hatch rate.

Moments before setting the eggs inside an incubator, first, expose them to room temperature for an hour or two. They should be clean, fertile, fresh, and free of abnormalities.

Float Testing Eggs to Determine the Level of Freshness

In the event you can't candle the eggs to tell their level of freshness, you can simply fill a bowl with water (at room temperature), then one by one, put the eggs inside.

Fresh eggs will sink to the bottom and lie flat on their sides. Such fertile eggs yield high hatch rate. Carefully take them out of the water, wipe dry, and put them at room temperature to await incubation.

Those that are a few weeks old but still viable for consumption will sink but stand on one end at the bottom of the bowl. They may not yield great results when incubated.

Those that float on the surface of the water are no longer fresh for eating or incubation. Simply discard them away.

Chapter Nine

Incubation

Unlike fertile chicken eggs that take 21 days to hatch, a successfully incubated fertile quail egg may take 15 to 18 days to hatch.

How to Successfully Incubate Quail Eggs

Generally, quail eggs take an average of 17 to 24 days to hatch. However, there are emerging mutants of quail whose eggs may take an average of 14 to 15 days to hatch.

Since most domesticated quail lack that ability to go broody, the ideal way to hatch their eggs is through use of an artificial egg incubator. Interestingly, quail eggs can be hatched by use of a number of commercially available egg incubators, though you must fittingly set the eggs in suitable trays, and suitably adjust the incubator to right conditions favorable to hatching the eggs.

When using any commercial egg incubator, go through the manufacturer's manual to familiarize yourself with how it functions.

Clean and disinfect the incubator thoroughly. Thereafter, pre-test its ability to provide the right temperature, correct humidity, and proper ventilation.

Temperature and Humidity

For any incubator to hatch quail eggs, it has to provide suitable temperature and relative humidity, Set the temperature inside the incubator at 37.5° ± 0.5°C (99.5° ± 0.5°F) with a relative humidity of 60% (the wet bulb reading should be at 30° ±0.5°C (86° ± 1.0°F). Maintain these until the 14th day of incubation.

In pursuit of relative humidity, many quail keepers do the mistake of adding too much water inside the incubator. I would strongly advise against adding more water during incubation to avoid over moisturising the incubation units.

Check these conditions at least twice a day, but avoid constantly adjusting the temperature once the eggs are inside. They can easily turn dud.

When using an electric enabled incubator but reside in a location prone to power blackouts, have a standby power back up like a generator to help maintain the incubator's temperature in case of an electric power blackout.

Subjecting the eggs to any prolonged unfavorable conditions inside the incubator can make them go stale instead of hatching!

Turning the Eggs

Once the eggs are correctly set in the incubator, ensure they are turned at least four times each 24 hours. This is vital to ensure uniform heating so that the embryo doesn't develop sticking to one side of the egg. You can develop your own egg-turning schedule, say like at 6am, 12pm, 6pm, and 12am.

Use of modern, fully automated and digital incubators comes with the advantage of enjoying the automatic egg-turning process. Although costly, these automatic incubators have programmed settings that make the whole incubation process flawless. But if you have to manually turn the eggs, ensure they are turned between 42-45degrees, through to 180 degrees according to your schedule.

Optimal turning is particularly critical during the first week of incubation to prevent early mortality. When turning the eggs, examine them for any damage. Get rid of those with cracks and leaking egg fluid since they will never hatch. In fact, even if the egg hatches, the resultant chick may never be as a healthy as the rest of the chicks.

Do not turn the eggs during the last 24 hours to hatching. No matter how tempting it might be, avoid opening the incubator after the 14th day, until the eggs have fully hatched and the baby chicks are dried and fluffy. This is vital in that the eggs need humidity generated by the live chicks inside to ease pipping, and subsequent egg shell breaking.

Ensure the incubator is cleaned thoroughly after each hatch.

Link for further reading

Various samples of Incubators:
https://www.backyardchickens.com/articles/homemade-chicken-egg-incubator-designs-pictures.47737/

Why Incubated Eggs May Fail to Hatch, and Possible Solutions for Each Case

Below are the six leading causes of poor egg-hatch inside an incubator and possible solutions for each case:

- ✓ **Incubation of infertile eggs**
  It would be deemed miraculous for an infertile egg to hatch a chick!

  Solution: Candle the eggs before and during incubation (before the 15th day) to help detect infertile eggs. But prior to that, correctly pair the males vs. the females to guarantee high fertility rate of the eggs.

- ✓ **Incubating defective/abnormal eggs**

As already shown, an egg may be regarded to be with a defect if it has cracks on its outer shell, its shell is contaminated, has the presence of a double egg yolk or absence of the yolk, has very dark spots or blood spots or bloody ring around or in its yolk.

Solution: Candle the eggs prior to incubation to ensure abnormal eggs do not see the inside of an incubator. Equally, collect eggs regularly (at least twice a day) and store them in a humid room with pointed ends facing downwards.

- ✓ **Failure to turn the eggs**

  The main reason for turning eggs during incubation is to guarantee uniform warming. Failure to do so may result into overheating of one part/one side of an egg thus rendering it unsuitable for hatching chicks.

  Solution: During incubation, commit to turning the eggs at least four times each24 hours. Equally, you can use an automatic egg incubator with a proven ability to turn eggs at the required angels.

- ✓ **Lack of favorable conditions inside the incubator**

  As already noted, for a fertile quail egg to be effectively hatched, the incubator has to provide: suitable temperatures, relative humidity and adequate fresh air.

- ✓ **Solution**: Use egg incubators with proven ability to hatch eggs. Equally, clean and disinfect the incubator before use. And if you reside in an area which experiences several power failures, have a power back up to guarantee smooth functioning of the incubator (in the absence of electric power supply).

- ✓ **The eggs may appear fertile when candled but still fail to hatch**
  This could be a result of incubating eggs from older hens. Equally, it could be a result of incubating eggs which have taken too long after being laid (those over ten days old).

- ✓ **Solution:** Always incubate eggs from younger and mature breeds of quail. Equally, incubate eggs at 7-8 days old and below. Desist from holding laid eggs for longer than 8 days in the storage facility as this may greatly lower their hatch rate. Avoid washing dirty eggs with water. Doing so may block the natural egg's protective layer and expose it to entry by organisms, thus hampering its hatchability. And before placing the eggs in an incubator, store them at room temperature.

- ✓ **Poor management of the egg incubator**
  Poor control of temperatures and humidity inside the incubator can be disastrous to egg hatching. Unclean and poorly disinfected incubator may too contribute to poor egg hatching.

✓ **Solution**: Ensure the incubator offers the right and consistent temperatures and humidity throughout the incubation period. Have the incubator placed inside of a room where no change in temperature and humidity can easily occur. Equally, take time to clean and disinfect it before and after use.

Pipping

Pipping is when a chick is trying to break through the egg shell at hatching. First, you'll observe an *internal pip* – a dent on the egg shell protruding inside out. It's created when the chick pecks on the inside of the egg shell. It's not clearly visible on the outside, but you might hear the chick chirping at this stage.

The comes *zipping* – which is an elaborate circular or straight line or opening on the egg. Once the chicks *unzip*

enough, they eventually come out of the egg shell. At this stage, the chirping sound would be more clear.

Pipped Eggs That Fail to Hatch

The moment an embryo develops to the pipping stage, or at first egg shell cracking at hatching, they are normally healthy enough to hatch unless affected by poor ventilation and inappropriate humidity inside the incubator.

The air exchange requirement inside the incubator is generally high during the last day of incubation. Moments before hatching, the chicks begin breathing using respiratory system thus necessitating an increase in oxygen requirement.

Don't decrease ventilation openings at hatching in an attempt to increase humidity. Too much humidity during incubation or little humidity during the hatching period can cause mortality to the developing embryo, and to the impending chick respectively.

How to Float Test Eggs that Fail to Hatch

Ever tried float testing to tell if an egg is too old to eat? You can use a similar test on eggs that haven't hatched to ascertain if there are still live chicks inside or not.

You've got to be extra careful when doing float testing. First, wait until most of the eggs have hatched. Waiting say 24 hours after the last chick comes out would be ideal. Then closely examine the remaining eggs to make sure none is pipped or has cracks. You may accidentally drown a chick if you do float testing on a pipped egg!

Now fill a transparent container with clear water, the temperature of a baby bottle (I normally use a large-sized transparent plastic cup). Allow the water to settle in the container, then take an egg out of the incubator and carefully lower it into the water.

If the egg sinks to the bottom of the container, it's a suggestion it was infertile from the beginning and now worth discarding. If the egg floats, closely take a look at the floating pattern: If it's floating with the pointed end facing downwards with the big end sticking up above water (vertically), that egg may have been infertile from the start or may have died within the first few days. If the egg is floating on its side (horizontally), it's a suggestion a live chick could still be inside. Carefully take it out of the water, wipe it dry, and take it back in the incubator for a day or two. In fact, an egg with a live chick may start to move around the water on its own.

Doing float testing may help you help you avoid getting the late hatching eggs out of the incubator before their due date, and possibly boost your hatch rate.

Chapter Ten

Taking Care of Quail Chicks

Whether you hatch your own quail eggs or plan on rearing day-old chicks, you'll need to plan for the critical first few days of their lives.

Once the chicks are dry and fully fluffed, transfer them to a brooder. Some will fluff up within an hour, while others may take longer. The fluffing is necessary to enable them stay warm.

Quail chicks are sensitive to a number of things. Without careful handling, they may register high mortality rate at that stage. And given that they are tiny, they resultantly can easily escape from their enclosure, get hurt by any dangerous object, or get injured by other animals. You must therefore administer high standards of care and management when handling them.

Brooder

You can purchase a commercially available brooder from most stores. You can as well use a cardboard box to make a perfect brooder (if raising the birds on a small scale).

Keep the brooder warm, dry, safe, and sanitary. Any exposure to prolonged cold may make the chicks suffer hypothermia and die.

Its corners should be round to prevent the chicks from pilling at them.

If you have some extra space in your room/home, you can set the brooder there. You can as well place it at a garage or at a shade - as long as that place is secure, safe, dry, warm, and away from predators and domestic pets like dogs and cats.

Temperature

During the first week, you can use a heat lamp to keep the temperature at between 32.2^0C-37.8^0C (90^0F-100^0F) - have a thermometer placed inside the brooder to check this. Thereafter, lower the temperature by 5^0c each week, until room temperature is realized (4-5 weeks later).

Observing the behavior of chicks inside the brooder

You can observe the movement and behavior of the chicks inside the brooder to help you tell the prevailing temperature. If the temperature is low, the chicks will be seen surrounding the heat source, with some jumping on others' flaps. Presence of high or too much temperature will force the chicks to move away from the heat source, while others will be seen panting, going mute or looking scared.

Lighting

During the first and second week, ensure 24 hours access to light. In the third week, reduce the light to 14 hours a day.

Note: You can rely on weather and climatic conditions to correctly set the temperature and lighting conditions inside the brooder.

Bedding

Use paper towel as bedding for the first three weeks then change to wood shavings thereafter (after the birds have learnt how to separate their feeds from the beddings).

Keep the chicks in the brooder for between 3-4 weeks. Thereafter, you can transfer them to the cages.

Feed Management

Up until they attain 4 weeks, give the chicks finely ground non-medicated turkey starter of game bird starter. They need high protein content from the word go!

Always ensure the feeds are in small/fine particles for the chicks to consume!

Give them plenty of clean fresh water (at room temperature). You should have the water bowl cleaned on a daily basis to prevent the water from getting dirty, and to equally prevent any bacteria from entering the bowl.

If the bedding appears messier, have the bowl cleaned at least twice a day.

Give them water in a shallow bowl, and ensure they can comfortably access it. For deep bowls, add some glass or stone pebbles to prevent the chicks from drowning - in the unfortunate event they step in.

Clean the brooder on a daily basis and ensure it doesn't have big spaces that can allow the chicks easy passage out.

Links for further reading

1. Hatching Quail Eggs and Brooding Quail Chicks
https://www.backyardchickens.com/articles/hatching-quail-eggs-and-brooding-quail-chicks.67362/

2. How to take Care of Quail Chicks
https://www.wikihow.com/Care-for-Quail-Chicks

Chapter Eleven

Quail Health

This section has been contributed by Francis Okumu; the famous author of Quail **Farming for Beginners – Everything You Need to Know**

Although quail are hardy birds, they occasionally get infected by certain diseases.

General Signs Exhibited by Sick Quail

Any sick quail will tend to exhibit some of the below signs:

✓ Numb, un-alert and unresponsive

Sick quail may appear numb and un-alert. They may appear unresponsive to touch, and will mostly be seen sleeping on the floor of their housing. But if standing, they will be exhibiting a weakling posture.

✓ Reduction in productivity

If there is sudden reduction in the number of eggs laid by the hens, that could be a possible sign of disease infection, or stress.

✓ Very high or very low body temperatures

Occasionally, check the body temperatures of your quail to establish if any could be exhibiting very high or very low temperatures. Such could be a sign of disease infection.

✓ Lack of appetite

Sick quail tend to lack normal appetite and as a result, will end up consuming lesser quantities of feeds when compared to the quantities they do normally feed on.

✓ Weight loss

Due to lack of appetite, a sick quail may register weight loss and begin to appear weak, dehydrated and pale-faced.

✓ Lackluster behavior

Sick quail may appear gloomy and disinterested even when you give them feeds, water or special treats like mealworms.

- ✓ **Observable defects in defecations**

When the defecation appears bloodstained, that's a sure sign of internal infection. If it has an accompaniment of worms, that's a sign of parasitic infection. If it is very hard, or very watery, such could be signs of dehydration, and diarrhea, respectively.

- ✓ **Difficulty in breathing**

Blocked mucus membranes, or any observable or hearable sound indicating some difficulty in breathing by any bird could be a sign of a respiratory disease infection.

- ✓ **Loose plumage**

If the feathers are falling off, or appear rough in texture, be sure to closely check the affected bird for possible disease infection.

Note: Once you identify any sick bird, you need to isolate it with speed from the rest of the flock. Afterwards, seek for the services of a trained poultry vet to help you effectively diagnose and possibly treat the affected bird.

Always desist from trying to treat any sick quail on your own if you aren't sure about the disease or infection the bird might be suffering from.

What Makes Quail to Be Susceptible to Disease or Pest Infection

Below are some of the leading factors making quail to be susceptible to disease or pest infections.

1. **Age**

   Did you know that older quail are usually prone to disease infections? This is due to their weakened body defense mechanisms. Equally, younger quail too, are prone to infection by certain diseases due to their not-fully-developed body immune system.

2. **Physical injuries**

   Any physical injury on any part of a quail's body may make it susceptible to bacterial infection. Such injuries may be inflicted by other quail, quail owner, or even by the affected quail.

3. **Environment**

   Very cold or very chilly weather conditions may make it possible for quail to contract respiratory diseases like pneumonia.

4. **Sex**

   Did you know that due to their frequencies in laying eggs, hens are more delicate and more prone to disease infection as compared to roosters?

5. **Poor sanitation**

   Unhygienic housing conditions may spur an outbreak of certain contagious diseases like Coccidiosis.

6. **Mixing of other poultry breeds with quail**

   This too may easily facilitate spread of contagious diseases within the flock. If you mix quail and chicken in the same housing, any chicken suffering from a disease like say histomoniasis may easily transmit it to quail.

The Four Most Common Quail Diseases, Preventions and Treatments

An average quail farmer may not clearly identify and offer an effective diagnosis and treatments to quail diseases at the farm level without relevant training, experience and equipment. Specifically, without training and proper equipment, it would be difficult to diagnose internal infections.

Quail are hardy birds known to be resistant to a number of diseases affecting poultry birds. Interestingly, lots of research on diseases affecting quail is ongoing and hopefully, future quail bird farmers will have a broader knowledge on dealing with the most common and emerging quail diseases.

Below are the four most common quail diseases, preventions, and treatments.

1. Coccidiosis

Coccidiosis is a parasitic infection which has a severe effect on the digestive tracts of infected quail birds. It normally attacks quail which are less than 7 weeks old. (Birds beyond 7 weeks of age are usually resistant to coccidiosis, but in cases of attack, the impact is usually not as severe as it is to birds below 7 weeks of age).

Since coccidiosis affects the digestive tracts of the birds, the infected birds would generally slow down and eventually stop eating. They will subsequently grow weak, pale and weak legged. If not attended to on time, the infected birds may die.

Prevention and treatment

Coccidiosis affects quail and other poultry birds out of poor management of farms i.e. failure to keep the poultry houses clean and dry. Coccidiosis thrives where there is a buildup of wet quail droppings and in moist areas around water points and feeders.

You therefore need to ensure the cages are dry and free of wet quail droppings. It's advisable constructing the areas around feeders and water points using wire mesh. This ensures no quail dropping accumulates within the cages.

Certain quail feeds are laced with coccidiostat; a drug that helps prevents infection by coccidiosis. To the birds which are not yet infected with coccidiosis, the consumption of coccidiostat in the feeds allows them limited infection with coccidiosis, and thereafter, they develop immunity against the disease. Also, consult an experienced poultry vet for recommendation of the best anticoccidial to use to contain coccidiosis.

2. Worms (Capillary Worms/Thread Worms/Crop Worms)

The second disease or rather parasite which affects quail is worms. Specifically, the most dangerous of the worms are those that infect the lining of the birds' crop(s). Capillary worms, scientifically known as *Capillaria spp.* falls in this category.

The infection caused by capillary worms can never be diagnosed by merely looking at the bird physically. It's only when the crop of an infected bird is removed, or when the crop of a bird which has died of the infection is removed and opened, then worms which appear thread-like can be seen lining across the tissue fragments of the bird's crop.

The infected birds often eat a lot, but always appear as if starving. And in the last stages of infection, the infected birds may experience difficulty in breathing, and defecations of infected birds may have accompaniments of worms. These are the three most common physical symptoms of a bird infected with capillary worms.

Prevention and treatment

Capillary worms usually thrive in wet droppings and in wet areas around feeders and waterers. The best way to control infection and spread of capillary worms is by constructing the base of the birds' cages with wire mesh. Spaces on the wire mesh would not allow build-up of quail' wet droppings and thus, will prevent the birds from picking the disease from the cages, and lessen its spread, if any. The cages too should be raised from the ground.

To treat capillary worms, it is recommended you use a correct wormer (de-wormer). Consult an experienced poultry vet within your area for recommendation on an appropriate wormer (de-wormer), since the names of these drugs differ from one country to another.

3. Histomoniasis

This is one of the most lethal diseases affecting quail. Histomoniasis, also known as a blackhead, is a protozoan infection which attacks a number of poultry breeds. In fact, it is usually referred to as a disease of the larger fowl unit.

Histomoniasis infects the liver of quail and immediately, starts to produce necrotic lesions which eventually results into fatal liver damages of the infected birds. The infected birds often exhibit restlessness, poor appetite, loss of feathers, and sulfur-like colored droppings.

Prevention and treatment

It is believed chickens which have recovered from histomoniasis are its carrier. Therefore, as a precautionary measure, avoid mixing chickens with quail birds under the same housing.

For treatment purposes, use relevant wormers (de-wormers), to help eliminate cecal worms which transmit histomoniasis. However, the most effective treatment for histomoniasis lies in its prevention.

4. Ulcerative Enteritis

Ulcerative enteritis is another destructive quail disease. From its name, the disease occurs like an ulcer on the internal linings of the infected birds' intestines. However, the most effective way to diagnose Ulcerative enteritis is through laboratory analysis.

The disease can easily be transmitted from one infected bird to another through contact with the droppings of the infected bird. It has too been established that birds which have recovered from ulcerative enteritis are usually its carrier.

Prevention and treatment

The most effective ways to prevent spread of this fatal disease lies in exercising clean sanitary measures and in the quick identification and quarantine of the infected birds.

Clean up the cages off any wet droppings, and it is essential the holding areas of the cages be built with wire mesh to help stop any accumulation of the birds' wet droppings.

For treatment, liaise with an experienced poultry vet for recommendations on effective drugs to use.

Note: Before administering any diseases control, it's vital to first consult a veterinary practitioner for guidance.

Remarkable link for further reading

Quail Diseases, Health Issues and Keeping Your Quail Healthy*https://www.backyardchickens.com/articles/quail-diseases-health-issues-and-keeping-your-quail-healthy.67379/*

Chapter Twelve

More on Quail Health

Bumblefoot

When using wire mesh as the floor of the cage, ensure it's smooth and with very tiny spaces – it shouldn't allow quail's foot to slip in and get trapped. Using a wrong wire mesh may easily make the birds susceptible to **bumblefoot infection.**

If quail are constantly walking on hard or rough surface, they can develop small lumps or wounds on the bottom of their feet - bumblefoot. Bumblefoot is characterized by lesions, and swelling of the infected foot pad. If the infection is left untreated, it may turn fatal! These wounds can heal over time, but may leave some infection. You'll have to use the right antibiotic for treatment. And lancing would be necessary for any surface swellings, so it's vital to consult a trained vet.

Bumblefoot may exist in three stages. The first stage is characterized by a small shiny patch on the foot of the bird. This is largely caused by wrong perching, perching for too long, or due to hard beddings. In the second stage, the infection usually has penetrated the skin. And in the third stage, the bird's foot may exhibit distortion of the contours of the foot- resulting into considerable damage.

Treating Bumblefoot

When it's at the third stage, it's advisable to seek for services of trained avian vet since corrective surgical operation may be a necessity. However, you can manage to deal with the first and second stage infection by following the below simple procedure:

Requirements:
- Clean water at room temperature, or lightly warmed.
- A clean and dry towel.
- Antibiotic (you can use Duramycin 10 Tetracycline Hydrochloride soluble powder) You can get this from most local feed stores

Steps
- ✓ Do this in the evenings or at night - when the bird is well fed and relaxed.

- ✓ Make a paste out of the Duramycin 10 by mixing it with water in a glass, bowl or cup. There is no specific measurement, just mix the powder with water until it forms a lump-free paste.

- ✓ Get the affected quail and clean its feet (wash with lightly warmed water and dry it up with a clean towel).

- ✓ Ensure you have a good grip on the bird, and then slowly cover the affected foot in good amount of paste.

- ✓ Once the foot if fully smothered in paste, hold the bird for at least 15 minutes for the paste to soak in.

- ✓ Afterwards, wash the bird's feet and dry it up with the towel. Then let it back in the housing.

- ✓ Do this every evening/night, until the infection is gone, and then again at least three more times after to ensure it's fully gone.

Note: In the absence of Duramycin 10, consult an experienced vet for the best alternative antibiotic to use, or for intervention.

You can also simply wash the infected foot in water mixed with iodine (every evening), dry it up, and then let the bird back in the housing. You should repeat this for at least seven days (until the infection disappears).

Toe-Balling

Toe-balling is simply a hard encrustation forming on the feet of quail due to the bird constantly walking on moist dirty litter (like moist dirty wood shavings mixed with quail waste).

Managing Toe-Balling

To remove the toe-ball, sock the foot in warm water till the encrustation softens, then carefully and softly, pick it away. Do this with lots of caution to avoid damaging the bird's foot, toe, or claw. And to limit toe-balling, raise the hygiene standards within the birds' housing.

Also note that if the birds are constantly walking on frosty surfaces, they may encounter foot problems or damage, regardless of the hygienic standards of the housing.

Pest Management

Quail infected with mites, lice, flea and ticks may exhibit slowdown in egg production, may be less active, and may get engaged in feather plucking.

There are several treatments you can pursue to deal with these external parasites including use chemical based products available from most pet stores and feed stores. You can buy them in either spray or powder form.

Use of Permethrin

This is a known worldwide safe insect killer. It's largely used by many poultry owners around the world to contain parasites such as lice and mites and can also be safely used to spray the quail's cage to get rid of the parasites.

When the cages are infested with the parasites, the quail will soon get infested with the parasites too. Once you clean the quail, it's necessary to disinfect the cage as well. Spay the permethrin in cracks, bedding, water troughs and feeders. Thereafter, remove all the bedding and then clean the feeders and waterers. Then wash the cage thoroughly, while scrubbing the floor, the corners, and all the surfaces.

Use of Garlic

Garlic is believed to be a good lice/mite/flea killer when mixed in right proportions with water and essential oil. Make a solution by mixing I ounce of garlic, 10 ounces of water, and a teaspoon full of essential oil. You can also use the same mixture to disinfect quail's housing.

Garlic

General Things You Can Do to Contain Quail Pests and Diseases

Always raise the birds under sanitary conditions. The moment you choose to raise your birds negligently, under unsanitary conditions, be rest assured that in case of any disease outbreak, even the best of drugs when administered may be rendered ineffective. Raising quail under sanitary conditions is your first step towards containing common quail pests and diseases.

Ensure the birds' house is always clean and properly disinfected. Wet and uncollected quail' droppings around water points and feeding zones may expose the birds to deadly infections like Coccidiosis.

Dust the birds occasionally with appropriate pesticides to keep external parasites away.

Their house should be well constructed to shield the birds from wind, hot sun, rodents like snakes, and other domestic pets like cats and dogs. This is now a song!

Construct their house with cold insulators to keep their house warm during winter, and provide enough ventilation to cool down the house during hot summer. Equally, the house should have adequate exposure to light (natural or artificial).

Always feed quail on quality and well-balanced diet, containing the right amounts of nutrients needed by the birds. If done right, the birds will reward you with quality eggs and meat, coupled with hardy birds resistant to a number of diseases.

Give the birds clean and fresh water for drinking, placed at strategic positions where they do not need any unnecessary strain to access to it. It is usually advisable to give them water at room temperature. Avoid giving them very cold or very hot water as they will avoid drinking such.

When some quail begin to physically appear weak or gloomy, isolate them from the rest of the flock, as fast as you can, and closely observe them for any possible illness.

De-worm the birds regularly using recommended de-wormers to prevent infestation by worms and other protozoan diseases.

Quarantine and de-beak any noted cannibal within the flock to bar them from inflicting wounds on other birds - which may subsequently make the wounded birds be susceptible to bacterial infection.

Avoid mixing quail of different age groups within the same accommodation to curb older birds molesting the younger ones.

Use of Apple Cider Vinegar

Giving the birds water laced with apple cider vinegar (ACV) has numerous health benefits, and most importantly, helps in boosting their immune system. It's handy when the birds are stressed which can cause them to slow down on normal activities and develop low immune system.

Dosage

Add the apple cider vinegar to the drinking water once a week, or alternatively four times straight days every month. Use ¾ to 1 table spoon per gallon of water. The water container should be plastic and must be dry and clean before use. Use of metal container can result in release of metallic salts that can end up harming the birds.

Due to the acidic content of apple cider vinegar, it can also be used as an effective antiseptic and antibiotic. It has the potential of killing germs.

Once you disinfect waterers and feed troughs with a detergent, you can rinse them in water containing apple cider vinegar. Its use also helps in controlling worms in quail.

You can buy the apple cider vinegar from stores, or prepare one at home.

DIY –How to Make Homemade Apple Cider Vinegar

The process of making homemade apple cider is quite simple. First, get the below items:

- Apples (5- 10)
- Sugar (organic cane sugar)
- Glass container (jar)
- Fresh water
- Cheesecloth or coffer filter
- Rubber band

Wash the apples, dry them up and chop into medium sized pieces. (You can also use the apple peels)

Put the chopped pieces in a glass jar.

Mix sugar with a cup of water and pour on top of the chopped apples – until the apples are completely submerged.

Then cover the jar with cheesecloth or coffee filter and then secure it with a rubber band.

Store the jar in a dark place at room temperature disturbance-free location to ferment.

You can check it after 3-4 days to ensure the apples are under water and that no mold is building up. During the time, you can also stir it with some clean and dry wooden ladle.

After 2-3 weeks, strain the apple pieces out and retain the liquid in the jar for another 2-3 weeks.

After the three weeks, you can test the vinegar to ascertain if it has acquired the acidity level you want, then transfer it to a bottle with a lid – and begin using it.

Can You Give Baby Quail Apple Cider Vinegar?

Yes you can, but ensure you keep it at minimum (½ to ¾) table spoon per gallon of water. Since ACV is full of vitamins, minerals and trace elements, it will help the chicks grow strong and healthy.

Summarized Key Benefits of Keeping Healthy Quail

Production of high quality eggs and meat. I'm sure you may not want to see your quail lay eggs with attachments of any parasitic larvae, or worm infested meat. You want them to produce clean and fresh eggs and meat.

Healthy quail have inability to spread any contagious diseases among themselves, and even to human beings.

Healthy quail are vibrant, mature fast and have a longer lifespan. They are generally associated with high productivity.

Healthy quail are cost-effective to raise. You'll have minimal to no bills related to their treatment.

Unlike sick quail, healthy quail have a higher market value; they fetch higher prices.

Chapter Thirteen

General Care and Management

Quail chick

How to Hold Quail

Quail are shy, yet curious and charismatic birds. My daughter describes them as being 'flighty and shy'. When startled, they will immediately take a flight in a vertical manner (upwards). They are notorious for this. As a result, ensure you have a good grip when holding them as they will attempt to kick off with their feet and flap their wings vigorously in an attempt to escape from your hands.

However, their limbs are generally delicate, so hold them with care.

Once quail escape, they are generally hard to find and retrieve. They have mastered how to disguise themselves once they escape.

To get a firm grip on the bird, slide the bird's neck between your index and middle finger, and put the rest of your fingers under its body. You can also turn the bird upside down while holding it in the same position – but not for too long (to avoid over-disorienting the bird).

Desist from holding the birds with their feet or legs, the limbs can easily break. Equally, avoid squeezing the area around the rib cage since you can easily break it.

Taming Quail

You can tame quail from an early age by hand feeding them tasty treats. As already indicated you can give them mealworms as the birds find them more appetizing.

When you begin taming the birds, exercise lots of patience. Give the treat in an open hand

Remember quail are not pets, they are game birds!

Approach them in a relaxed manner, avoiding eye contact in the initial stages(they do find eye contact intimidating).Keeping calm when approaching their accommodation will help you carry every day jobs with ease whilst keeping the birds relaxed as well.

You can also try talking to them in a soothing voice (they will take no time before recognizing your voice). They detest loud noises and unfamiliar faces.

You can consider putting on similar cloth when attending to the birds; they will readily recognize you and accord you a relaxed response.

You can try different colours, avoiding the ones they seem to dislike. Truth is, quail do take a dislike to certain colors, especially the bright colours. Some bright colors may signify danger to the.

Avoid putting on clothes with pictures of predators and domestic animals such as snakes, dogs, cats, foxes, etc. Such may instinctively remind them of danger.

Why Quail Fight and Possible Solutions for Each Case

Although quail may appear shy – with fragile limbs and chubby bodies, they can easily pick a fight with one another, releasing a fury of feathers, breaks and claws in the process.

But why would they get engaged in a battle given that they are social birds in nature.

Below are some of the reasons why quail may pick a fight, and possible solutions for each case:

- **Overcrowding**

When too many birds are housed in a limited space, they will want to fight for the feeds, water, and for space.

Solution: Put the correct number of birds in each housing. Overcrowding will not only push them into endless fighting, but will also negatively affect their productivity.

- **Putting differently aged birds in the same housing**

Adult quail are territorial by nature. They may attack quail of lesser age when mixed together.

Solution: When housing the birds, always put those of the same age group in the same housing.

- **Bringing in of new birds**

Since quail are territorial by nature, new birds brought in may want to pick a fight with the existing flock just to show their 'might'. On the other hand, you may be unlucky to bring in new birds with fighting habits.

Solution: When you introduce birds to an existing flock, take time to monitor how they get along. In the event you notice any aggressive bird, isolate it from the rest of the flock.

- **Mixing of different quail breeds in the same housing**

Sometimes quail may want to pick a fight with one another simply because of difference in colour of their plumage, or due to difference in physically appearance.

Solution: When housing quail, ensure those of similar breed are put together in the same housing.

- **Incorrect ratio of male to female in the same housing**

When housing say twenty females with just one male in a room, they females may be tempted to pick a fight with one another over the male. Equally, when housing say twenty males with just one female in a room, the males may tend to pick a fight with one another over the female.

Solution: As already indicated, when housing both male and female quail together, the best ration would be 1 male to 3-4 females. This would not only help lower the urge of females to want to fight, but also result into higher fertilization of the eggs laid.

- **Raising of one sex in the same accommodation**

Male quail are prone to pick a fight with one another when housed together. This tendency emanates naturally from their territorial nature.

Solution: If you must house quail of same sex together, closely monitor the birds and isolate those showing aggressive tendencies.

- **Competition for limited feeders and drinkers**

Presence of limited feeders and waters may make the birds fight for their access.

Solution: Ensure the feeders and waterers are adequate in number and placed at convenient locations where the birds don't strain to access them.

- **Infestation by parasites such as lice, tick, and flea**

Sometimes parasites may attack the birds in tender places where the birds can't scratch. Consequently, the affected birds tend to pick a fight with others in an attempt to lower the itching emanating from such infested areas.

Solution: Always raise the birds under sanitary conditions and occasionally de-worm and dust them with relevant pesticides.

- **Idleness**

An idle quail can easily turn destructive! When quail stay idle for long, they can easily pick a fight just to get busy.

Solution: Keep the birds busy most of the time by giving them sand tubs for taking sand baths. Equally, you can hang some green vegetables within their accommodation to keep them busy as they peck them.

- **Fighting for the fun of it**

When some quail are overly excited, they may want to pick a fight with others just for the fun of it.

Solution: Closely monitor the birds and identify the aggressive ones. If their aggressiveness persist or increases, isolate them from the rest of the flock.

Feather Plucking In Quail - Causes and Possible Solutions

Feather plucking is a very common problem in quail and it's caused by a variety of things. While some causes can be serious, others are minor.

Below is a list of some of the common causes of feather plucking, and possible solutions for each case:

- **Mating**

When quail are mating, the males are prone to peck and want to cling on the females' head. The situation can get worse if there are fewer females in the housing. If this could be the cause, then it will be evident by only the females getting bald while the males are looking ok.

Solution

Always pair the males and females accordingly. This will reduce the frequency of one female being pecked on the head over and over.

- **Fighting**

Quite may often tend to pick a fight - especially the male ones. The fights are largely territorial, but in other instances, they may engage in a battle for food, water, space, and sometimes just for the fun of it. It's also possible to have a female bully within the flock.

When engaged in a battle, quail do pull each other's feathers. Within their accommodation, you can easily spot the bully and the victims – the bully's feathers are usually intact while the victims have missing feathers.

Solution

One way of lowering fighting tendency in quail is via de-beaking birds with sharply pointed beaks. Equally, closely monitor the bully and if the fighting persists, then isolate it from the rest of the flock (but keep in mind that quail are social birds – should be paired with another). And most importantly, provide the birds with sufficient amount of feeds in adequate feed troughs (bowls).

- **Infestation by mites, lice, ticks, and flea**

These parasites cause an itching effect on the areas they attach themselves on – as they draw blood from their host. To contain the itching, quail are forced to peck at the affected areas, thereby plucking the feathers.

Solution

Always raise the birds under sanitary conditions and dust them with relevant pesticides every two to three months. Also, give them a place to take sand bath. Sand bathing will help them get rid of the external parasites - it's quail's way of cleaning themselves.

- **Lack of enough nutrients in the feeds**

Quail need feed rich in protein. In the event you give them feeds containing less protein, they will tend to peck their own feathers in pursuit of the missing protein.

Solution

Feed the birds on nutritious and well balanced diet. Being game birds, game bird feeds or turkey feeds has the relevant protein content they need. Also treat them to mealworms, bugs, and some green vegetable, and when they begin laying eggs, you can grind oyster shells and give them.

- **Stress**

When quail are stressed, they may slow down or stop from feeding and from engaging in daily activities. Resultantly, they will begin losing weight and shedding feathers. And it can get worse if the cause of stress is not resolved quickly. Many things cause stress in quail including predators, noise, disturbance, excessive cold, limited feeds, inadequate space, overcrowding etc.

Solution

Identify the cause of stress and solve it - as fast as you possibly can. Always raise the birds in noise/disturbance-free environment, shield them from access by predators, shield them from cold during winter, give them adequate feeds and enough space, and raise the right number of birds in the right structure.

- **Rough surfaces inside their housing**

Could there be some rough or pointed wires or nails inside the birds' accommodation that could be pricking their feathers? When quail are startled, they tend to immediately jump straight up, and can easily damage their heads and feathers inside their housing.

Solution

Build or buy an appropriate house for the quail. Ensure it's safe and secure. It should be free from loose wires and nails, and provide padding on the top the cage. When quail are startled and jumps upwards, the padding will shield their heads and feathers from potential harm.

Pecking in Quail – Causes and Possible Solutions

Pecking in quail is largely a behavioral problem. If not checked, it may turn into cannibalism, where the culprit consumes all or part of another bird as food or just for the fun of it.

But what are the leading causes of pecking in quail?

- ✓ **Inbreeding**

    When a quail is a product of parents with pecking disorder, they can easily acquire the bad habit genetically, or by observing their parents.

- ✓ **Accident**

  Sometimes quail may start pecking others by accident, due to idleness, or merely to show superiority. And if not checked, this may grow into a permanent habit.

- ✓ **Overcrowding**

  When many birds are housed in a tiny set up, they may start to peck each other in attempt to access feeds, water and space. Since quail are territorial by nature, overcrowding also makes the younger birds susceptible to molestation by older birds, including endless pecking.

- ✓ **Unbalanced feeds**

  Lack of necessary nutrients such as protein and calcium to the layers may make them peck each other in pursuit for the nutrients.

- ✓ **Unsanitary housing**

  Raising the birds in dirty housing, or failure to change their dirty bedding on time may expose them to attack by pests like mite and lice. Birds infested with such pests may resort to pecking others out of stress, or in attempt to get rid of the pests.

- ✓ **Mixing quail of different type**

Although quail are social birds, they feel more comfortable around other quail of same type (color, size, and type). They may attempt pecking those looking different.

How to Control Pecking in Quail

You can put in place the below measures to contain pecking problems in quail

- Closely observe the birds and identify any aggressor (with pecking tendency). If the habit continues, isolate it from the rest of the flock. You can sell it, give it away, or pair it with birds they get along with.
- You can also identify and de-beak birds with pecking tendency.
- Raise the birds under sanitary conditions. Give them a tub of sand to take sand-bath, and you can occasionally dust them with relevant pesticides to contain mites and lice.
- Always raise the right number of birds in the right kind of structure. Raise birds of the same age, colour, size, and type on the same space.
- Give quail well balanced feeds rich in protein and plenty of clean water for drinking.
- Keep the birds busy by hanging green vegetables in the housing. Also treat them occasionally to mealworms and other edible bugs.

Egg Eating in Quail

Egg-eating is also another devastating habit your quail can develop. Simply imagine going out to collect fresh eggs, only to find the quail have smashed them to pieces and eaten all of them!

So why would quail eat their own eggs?

Causes of Egg-Eating

- ✓ **Lack of adequate calcium/protein in diet**

Quail are sensitive towards detecting insufficient nutrients in their feeds, largely calcium and protein. If they are getting the two in inadequate quantities, they may begin looking elsewhere for them, and unfortunately, their eggs would come in handy if within their sight.

- ✓ **Accident**

Quail can accidently break an egg when startled, or when fighting. Once a broken egg is within their reach, they can be tempted to peck at it, and end up developing the unfriendly habit.

- ✓ **Stress/Nervousness**

When stressed or when nervous, quail can sometimes turn restless, and end up pecking at their own eggs just to find something to do to cool down. They can equally break the eggs when trying to duck for cover away from a predator.

- ✓ **Over-bright light in the nesting boxes**

Presence of over-bright light in the nesting boxes may get the birds overly-excited and skittish. Resultantly, they may be tempted to peck at their own eggs for the fun of it.

Identification

If you have a number of hens and can't tell the one with egg-eating habit, you can rely on the below signs to identify her:

Ensure the housing is securely shielded from access by predators. You must first rule out predators or external cause.

You may find traces of the sticky yellow yolk on the beak, legs, and feathers of the culprit.

Closely monitor the nesting points during egg-laying time (in the afternoons) - those with egg eating habit will want to hang around laid eggs for long.

Closely monitor the points where each hen prefers laying their own eggs. You may find broken egg shells and spilled yolk at the bottom of the nesting points preferred by the egg eaters.

You can also be lucky to catch the notorious egg eating bird in the act, accidentally.

Remember, it takes just one hen to influence the whole flock into egg eating!

Control of Egg-Eating

Ensure the feeds contain adequate protein and calcium to meet the birds' requirements. You can give them supplementary feeds such as well-grounded oyster shells, live mealworms and fresh vegetable (kales and spinach).

Collect the eggs frequently, once they are laid. Get hold of the eggs before the egg eating bird does.

You can also replace the laid eggs with dummies such as golf balls or plastic/wooden/glass/stone eggs - something similar yet hard (that will disinterest their pecking).

Ensure the nesting points are spacious, dark and private. They should not be overcrowded and brightly lit.

Should the egg eating bird persist, you can consider isolating her from the rest of the flock.

Worst case scenario, you might have to separate the naughty hen from the rest of the flock until all other hens have finished laying their eggs.

Chapter Fourteen

Why Your Quail are Dying, and Possible Solutions - Both Baby Quail and Adult Quail

Below are some of the possible reasons why your adult/baby quail are dying, and possible solutions for each case:

- **Chocking/Suffocation**

    When learning to eat, quail chicks can never tell the difference between their food and bedding materials like saw dust or wood shavings.

They may continuously peck on the bedding materials thinking it's food. They may fail to recognise a pile of food or dish of crumbles as food, while getting busy pecking at tiny things on the floor or walls of the brooder.

Equally, they may chock on feeds with large particles.

Solution

Use materials like folded newspapers as the bedding of the brooder at between 1-3 weeks. You can also use recycled paper kitty litter as bedding for between 1-3 weeks. Since most chicks have a watery paste attached to their tender feet when hatched (and it sometimes doesn't dry up immediately), the recycled paper kitty litter does the magic of drying up the watery substance. Using it also helps in telling when the water is spilled. Since it absorbs water, you can then remove the wet spots.

Give the birds finely ground starter feeds immediately they are hatched. They may have trouble eating the large-sized crumbs, and grinding the homemade crumbs into smaller particles may end up consuming your time.

Since quail are great scratchers, they may get the feeders and waterers filled with bedding particles easily. Therefore, change the feeders and drinkers frequently.

- **Sudden death**

You can wake up one morning to find a dead quail.

Solution

Have a post mortem done on the dead bird by a trained bird vet to ascertain the true cause of the death.

- **Drowning in drinking water**

The trickiest part in raising quail chicks is for them to learn how to eat and drink. If given water in deep bowls, they'll easily end up inside, and possibly drown.

Solution

Give them water in shallow bowls. If you must use deep bowls, then put in some glass or stone pebbles to prevent the chicks from drowning in case they step in.

- **Attack by rodents and predators**

Mice, rats, snakes and raccoons may attack quail and kill them in the process.

Solution

Ensure the birds' housing is safe and secure from access by rodents and predators.

- **Over-exposure to cold**

When the chicks are overly-exposed to cold, they may suffer hypothermia and die afterwards. The adult quail too would easily die during winter when exposed to cold. They may freeze to death.

Solution

Ensure the brooder has proper protection against cold and drought. You can use a 100W red reptile light - It has a good source of heat with a nice red light.

At 3 weeks, when the birds are nearly fully feathered, you can move them from the brooder to a bigger box with the heat source adjusted (further away – but still there).

Ensure the housing offers proper cover against cold – especially during winter. You can cover the housing with an old sack, add in more bedding materials, and introduce a heat lamp for the adult birds.

- **Disease outbreak**

Quail could be dying as a result of known or unknown disease outbreak.

Solution

Well, I would recommend you consult a properly trained vet to help you diagnose the type of disease, its cause, and prevention. And since there are few medications available for treatment of quail diseases, always exercise cleanliness, biosecurity, and proper sanitation of equipment.

- **Poor handling**

    Quail are more nervous than most poultry birds – they do not like being handled. When trying to catch them, they'll try hiding or jumping up. As a result, they may hit their head on a hard surface and die. Equally, since they may want wrestle away from your hands when holding them, you may unfortunately kill them by having a very tight grip. They may also accidentally slip from your hands and hit the ground hard enough and die.

    Solution

    A soft roof is recommended inside the birds' housing to shield them from hitting their heads hard when startled. Equally, approach the birds slowly, giving them space to scurry away before settling. And most importantly, give the birds a tender grip when holding them.

- **Fighting**

    Sometimes its death of one bird that may separate two quail that are entangled in a fight.

Solution

Raise differently aged birds differently to limit molestation of younger birds by older birds. You can also identify the aggressive birds within the flock and separate them from the rest.

- **Old age**

  Domesticated quail are known to live for $2_{1/2}$- 3 years. They may die afterwards due to old age.

  Solution

  There is little that can be done to stop any quail from dying due to old age. However, you can prolong their lives by giving them well balanced and nutritious feeds, and the right care and management.

- **Stress**

  Quail can get easily stressed by a number of things including change of location, presence of predators, introduction of new breed, noise, inhumane handling etc. If the cause of the stress persists, the birds can easily die.

  Solution

  Identify the cause of stress and eliminate it, as fast as you possibly can. Find the culprit, get rid of them and you'll end up keeping the birds stress-free.

Culling Quail – How to Butcher Quail

Quail culled through neck-twisting

There are several reasons for culling quail including; reducing the flock to manageable size, to get meat for the family table, to get rid of birds with undesirable qualities such as excessive cooing, feather picking, and egg pecking and so on.

There are two common ways of killing quail: twisting their head off, or chopping the head off using sharp knife, shear, or scissor.

The method you decide to use should be any method you feel comfortable with. When killing quail, do it in the quickest way possible to cause the least amount of stress not only to the birds, but also to yourself.

Location of the cull

Locate the cull away from the sight of unaffected birds, and away from the birds housing. During killing, other birds can easily pick up the sound of distress from the dying birds, and this can stress them.

Culling by chopping off the head

Hold the bird with a firm grip and then using a sharp knife, shear, scissor or any other cutting object, cut their head off. Once their heads are chopped off, old the bird upside down in a bucket...then wait for a minute or two, and it's done! It's that simple.

The bird may flap and wriggle, and may spill its blood all over your hands and body if you fail to hold it firmly.

Ensure the object you use in cutting the head of the bird is of good size, weight and sharp enough. It would be stressful failing to succeed on the first attempt given that quail skin is slippery!

Many quail owners have trouble killing quail for processing. The killing part freaks them out! When butchering Quail, think of the end product in mind, the meat. If you view them as birds, you might be tempted to back off.

You can get a strong willed family member, friend or worker to do the work if you are not emotionally strong.

You can then process and preserve quail meat in the same way as you would other poultry birds such as chicken.

Links for further reading

1. How to harvest quail for meat
https://www.gardenupgreen.com/2017/01/how-to-harvest-quail-for-meat.html

2. How I Process Quail
https://www.backyardchickens.com/threads/how-i-process-quail-my-6yr-old-helped-warning-graphic-pics.147712/

3. How to process quail (YouTube Video)
https://www.youtube.com/watch?v=rHXSnx4Htwk

Chapter Fifteen

Branding, Sales and Marketing

This chapter touches on things you can do to create a strong brand, and strategies you can utilize to market and sell your quail products.

How to Bolster Your Farm's Brand

If you were asked to randomly state at least five successful quail or poultry farms in the United States or anywhere else in the world, what are some of the names that would readily come into your mind? Texas quail farms, Manchester Farm, Circle L quail farm Inc., Quail haven Farm, Urgasa Quail Farm Inc.etc. are some of the farms that have readily come into my mind. These farms have built enviable memorable brands.

Most, if not all, successful quail farms started from scratch and have risen to be successful and solid business brands today. It's dedication, focus, hard work, and determination that has allowed the businesses to register such success. It's therefore no hidden secret that anyone can build a quail farm to be a successful brand anywhere in the world.

a. Get professional certifications

While you don't necessarily need any professional certification to start and run a quail farm, if you want your farm to stand out and make an impact, it's essential to acquire some of the relevant certifications. These certifications will not only validate your competency, they'll demonstrate your level of skill show commitment to a course you adore. They'll also demonstrate your 'up-to-date' level of indulgence in matters related to quail farming.

Some of these common certifications include: Certificate in poultry farming, Certificate in poultry production or management, Degree or Diploma in poultry production or management, etc.

b. Set favorable prices

In order to have an edge over your competitors, it's imperative to price your products favorably. And to help you realize this, the below will be handy:

- You can benchmark from your closest competitors' prices and set slightly low prices (mostly at market entry level). You can then later on adjust the prices accordingly to give you the right profit margins.

- Get your startup capital from sources that won't pile pressure on you, or from those sources that won't charge you high interest rates. This will help cushion you from wanting to sell the birds' products at throw away prices just to pay back the debts you owe.

- Get farm inputs, tools, equipment, and initial chicks from manufactures and wholesales - those offering some good discounts. Low input prices is key to coming up with the right pricing.

- Cut your operational costs to barest minimum.

- Put adequate cost- effective measures to effectively reach out to your target market. Put more cost-effective efforts in marketing/promotional activities.

- Utilize independent contractors and marketers to save on costs related to employing permanent sales and marketing personnel.

c. Promote your farm

To turn your farm into a reputable brand, you must be ready to invest in relevant and consistent promotions and advertisements.

Some of the strategies you can utilize are not limited to:

- ✓ Placing relevant adverts in both electronic and print media.

- ✓ Becoming a lead sponsor in relevant community-based or area-based events.

- ✓ Leverage on the internet to promote your farm. Utilize social media platforms such as Facebook, Twitter, Instagram, Google+, YouTube etc. to promote your quail farm.

- ✓ Erecting billboards with compelling message about your quail farm at strategic locations in your area, at the local market, at strategic locations within the city, and also at strategic locations around the country.

- ✓ Conduct road shows from time to time to woo potential households within the neighborhood. Utilize road shows targeting the local community to market and sell your quail products.

- ✓ Design fliers and brochures with compelling content about your quail farm and available products and distribute them to potential clients in strategic areas such as local markets, at local community gatherings including weddings and church functions.

- ✓ Create a website for your farm and employ strategies to help you pull relevant traffic (potential clients) to that site.

- ✓ Have branded shirts and caps worn by your employees. Equally, you can have a signage at the farm's gate (visible to the public), and the company's vehicles equally branded with the farm's logo.

- ✓ Hire sales people (occasionally) to reach out to potential customers (hotels, restaurants, food processing and packaging companies - those that need regular supply of quail products, food and grocery stores, supermarkets, hypermarkets, various local households etc.) and inform them about your quail farm together with available products, then seek to get a supply contract.

Simple Yet Effective Sales and Marketing Strategies

Since the capital requirement for starting small scale quail farming is generally low, you'll definitely encounter players in the quail farming industry in almost any place you set up your farm.

The level of competition may largely depend upon your location and the size of your farm. But with little add-ons such as processing and packaging, there are high chances of experiencing little to no competition.

When producing surplus eggs and meat, you can consider giving away, selling, or pickling for use at a later date.

When selling, it's advisable to first go through your own country's legislation to check the requirements.

In most countries, quail eggs and meat are covered by hygiene regulations and trading standards

When packaging, you can use a decorative and clearly marked label highlighting the name of your farm/business, contact details, and most importantly, the best before date.

You can also employ the below sales and marketing strategies to pull in potential customers.

- ✓ Build capacity. Before you go out sourcing to supply the bigger hotels, restaurants, and even larger households with quail products, it's essential to first build your capacity. Don't you think it would be embarrassing failing to consistently honor supply-related contracts you've signed due to low capacity on your end?

- ✓ Design a compelling company and personal profile that captures your qualifications, experience, and achievements; especially those related to quail farming. These will most definitely help boost your success when marketing and selling quail products.

- ✓ As already noted under brand promotion strategies, it's vital to re-emphasize the need of designing compelling introductory letters and brochures and send them to hotels, restaurants, households, food processing and packaging firms (those in need of quail eggs/meat), food stores, supermarkets and business in need of quail's products.

- ✓ Promptly send your bids for advertised tenders seeking supply of quail products.

- ✓ Engage in direct sales and marketing, personally. Equally, consider engaging the services of marketing executives and business developers to market and sell your quail's products.

- ✓ Encourage your satisfied customers, family members and friends to use word of mouth to refer other potential customers.

- ✓ Open the farm with some local party. This is one of the fastest ways of marketing it to the local residents.

- ✓ Utilize road shows targeting the local community to market and sell your quail products.

- ✓ Have your quail farm listed as an advertisement inside the yellow pages (local directory), and in local newspapers and magazines.

- ✓ Join local agribusiness groupings to help you network and market the products.

- ✓ Also, never forget to leverage on the internet to market and sell your quail products. Utilize social media platforms such as Facebook, Twitter, Instagram, Google+, YouTube etc. to continuously market the products.

THE END

Made in United States
Troutdale, OR
01/26/2024